Jim Henson's
Designs and Doodles

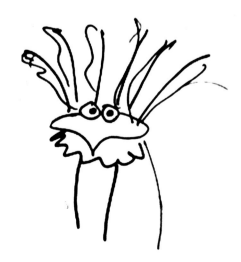

Jim Henson's

Designs and Doodles

A Muppet Sketchbook

by Alison Inches

Harry N. Abrams, Inc., Publishers

For Kermit the Frog, aka Jim

Editor: Ruth A. Peltason
Designer: Dana Sloan

Library of Congress Cataloging-in-Publication Data
Inches, Alison.
    Jim Henson's designs and doodles : a muppet sketchbook / Alison Inches.
        p. cm.
    ISBN 0-8109-3240-7
    1. Henson, Jim-Criticism and interpretation. 2. Henson, Jim-Notebooks,
sketchbooks, etc. I. Henson, Jim. II. Title.

    PN1982.H46 I53 2000
    791.5'3'092-dc21   00-22806

THE
Jim Henson
—COMPANY—

Printed and bound in Japan

Harry N. Abrams, Inc.
100 Fifth Avenue
New York, N.Y. 10011
www.abramsbooks.com

Contents

·· ❦ Acknowledgments ❧ ··

I am deeply grateful for everyone who helped make this book possible: The Henson family, with special thanks to Jane and Heather Henson. My crackerjack editor, Ruth Peltason. My friend and publisher, Jane Leventhal. The friends and colleagues of Jim Henson, who so dearly shared their time and thoughts with me: Jerry and Susan Juhl, Michael Frith, Kathy Mullen, Dave Goelz, Frank Oz, Bonnie Erickson, and Louise Gikow. And for those loving friends and family members, who supported me all the way: Robin Hoagland, Sally Hoagland, Rob Robertson, Ric McKown, and Mom.

And an extra-special thank you to Karen Falk, the Henson Archivist and Curator of the Designs and Doodles Exhibition, who was always at my right hand.

Alison Inches

···⊰ Foreword ⊱···

Jim Henson began his artistic career with the simplest of tools—a pencil and paper. When he moved on to film and television he continued, with enthusiasm and humor, to draw. He drew everywhere—in meetings, in restaurants, at home. Drawing, it might be suggested, was a way of thinking visually.

The artwork in this book comes from the collection of The Jim Henson Company Archives. Although not intended for posterity, these drawings allow us a rare peek into the imagination of a creative genius and brilliant innovator who brought delight and wonder to audiences around the globe.

The basis for this book was an exhibition that I curated in 1996 at the National Arts Club in New York City of some 100 drawings and watercolors, sponsored by The Jim Henson Legacy. Called, appropriately enough, "Jim Henson: Designs and Doodles," the exhibit was the first time the public could see original works by this immensely talented man. Now, five years later, it is extremely gratifying to see this exhibit revived and expanded in book form, giving an even greater audience an intimate look at Jim Henson's creative process.

The Jim Henson Legacy, founded in 1992, is a not-for-profit foundation dedicated to celebrating the life and work of Jim Henson. Many thanks are due to the Legacy, and in particular to Jane Henson, Arthur Novell, and Bonnie Erickson. Others who generously gave of their time are Richard Termine, Lauren Bien, Jerry Juhl, Michael K. Frith, Louise Gikow, and Craig Shemin. Because of these people, we are able to take these wonderful drawings from Jim's hand and put them into yours.

Enjoy!

Karen Falk
Archivist
The Jim Henson Company

Introduction

Before Kermit became "the Frog," he was an amphibious creature prone to donning a blond wig and lip-synching to Rosemary Clooney's "I've Grown Accustomed to Your Face." Rowlf—the piano-playing, canine king of puns—began his career as a quick-witted hound selling Purina Dog Chow in commercials and moonlighting on *The Jimmy Dean Show*. The yellow bird that once sang the praises of Royal Crown Cola was eventually transformed into Big Bird, the star of *Sesame Street*. And the shaggy monster with googly eyes, known as Cookie Monster, had a voracious appetite for computers before he developed a taste for cookies. These are some of the characters—drawn, built, and performed by Jim Henson—that came to be known as the Muppets.

But before these characters became Muppets, they were among scores of drawings and doodles jotted down in sketchbooks, on pads of paper, on letterheads, even on paper napkins. Like a Muppet family scrapbook, this collection of sketches documents the origins and development of Jim's characters. Ernie and Bert, in their earliest incarnation, appear as scribbles in marker on a piece of yellow-lined legal paper. The original Oscar the Grouch was purple rather than garbage green. An idea for a cigar-chomping king in a sketchbook comes alive as King Goshposh in an episode of the television special *Tales From Muppetland*. A cartoon strip drawn for a high school publication lays the groundwork for storyboards that introduce wacky humor into television commercials. And a doodle from the early sixties of an English-style music hall becomes the set for the international hit *The Muppet Show*.

Jim Henson left a paper trail of designs and doodles that lead back to his roots as a graphic artist. Not all of his early works on paper survive, but enough imagery exists to chart Jim's extraordinary imagination. Traced back to their origins, these drawings unveil his creations and reveal their creator.

Welcome to the world of *Jim Henson's Designs and Doodles*.

Opposite: *Short, round creatures, puppet designs.* 1960s. Pencil and ink on paper, 14 x 8½"
Below: *My Sketc-hbook,* first page of a sketchbook. 1962–70s. Ink and pencil, 8½ x 5½"

MY SKETC-
HBOOK

1962

JIM HENSON

Pages from a sketchbook. c. 1960. Sepia ink, 8½ x 11"

UP AND DOWN A SWAMPY RIVER:

Mississippi Childhood to College

"As children, we all live in a world of imagination, of fantasy, and for some of us that world of make-believe continues into adulthood."

—Jim Henson

Born on September 24, 1936, James Maury Henson spent his early years in Leland, Mississippi. He and his brother, Paul, often played along the banks of nearby Deer Creek, sometimes with neighborhood friends in tow. These back-yard excursions filled Jim Henson's mind with images of nature that would later appear in his sketchbooks as fanged snakes, buzzing dragonflies, and leaping frogs.

As a newlywed, Henson painted these images, now evolved into a band of colorful creatures, on the walls of his first home. Furry beasts came in different shapes and sizes, sometimes with horns, beaks, or claws, and all with pointed teeth and mischievous eyes. When Henson had children, he often worked on craft projects with them. They would each make their own Easter eggs, decorated with images of birds on spindly legs, butterflies and inchworms, and striped snakes; their Halloween pumpkins became glowing beast-o'-lanterns; even their cookie dough ornaments for the family Christmas tree had animal, monster, and alien shapes. Jim and his wife, Jane, painted designs on a hutch in their Greenwich, Connecticut, kitchen, and transformed a bathroom wall into a swirling mosaic of polka-dotted fish and spiraling flowers–both remain intact, fondly preserved by the current owners.

The images that Jim Henson first saw in nature would later become elabo-rate set designs for his television shows and movies. A southern swamp, complete with a full moon filtering through cypress trees, and fireflies, lighted by tiny flashlight bulbs, dotting the darkness, became the background for Linda Ronstadt's "Blue Bayou" on one of his shows. A river village built on top of wooden platforms became a wintry landscape where an otter named Emmet and his friends would form a memorable jug-band. A bog with real lily pads became the set for a dandy frog named Kermit to strum his banjo and sing "Rainbow Connection" in *The Muppet Movie*. All of these images can be traced back to Jim Henson's roots in the South. "The beauty of nature has been one of the greatest inspirations of my life," he once recalled. "Growing up as an artist, I've always been in awe of the incredible beauty of every last bit of design in nature."

Human nature also inspired Jim Henson's work. One of his earliest surviv-ing pieces of artwork is a silk-screened theater program for a high school pro-duction called *Nine Girls*. The girls are simple composite stick figures in triangle skirts, clustered around their stick-figure dance teacher. Using this simple form, Henson created an image that communicates the innermost thoughts of the characters. He would use this same simplicity with even greater effect in his later puppet designs. His characters would express the range of human emotions everyone feels. Theater programs such as this one, along with the skills he learned from constructing and painting sets for high school plays and dances,

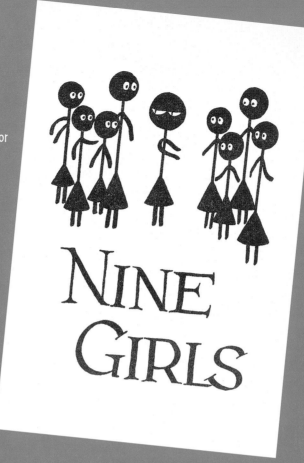

Nine Girls, program design for
a Northwestern High School
theater production. 1954.
Silkscreen, 9" x 6"

...⟨ Early Influences ⟩...

Over the years Jim Henson often made reference to the artists, entertainers, people, and forms of entertainment that influenced him. As a boy, Jim read classic fairy tales and such stories as *Winnie the Pooh*. An idea file in the archives at The Jim Henson Company reveals that he considered making James Thurber's *The Thirteen Clocks* into a show for television. Jim was also a big fan of Walt Disney's movies. Growing up, he delighted in the animation of *Dumbo, Pinocchio, Sleeping Beauty,* and *Fantasia,* as well as Disney's versions of *Alice in Wonderland* and, later, *Mary Poppins*. Another movie that deeply influenced Jim was *The Wizard of Oz*. He also loved the films of Jacques Tati, Alfred Hitchcock, Federico Fellini, and Ingmar Bergman. (A Muppets 3–D movie that still delights audiences at the Disney-MGM Studios theme park in Florida was one of the last projects Jim completed before his death in 1990.)

The characters in Walt Kelly's comic strip, *Pogo,* influenced Jim's development of Muppet characters. Some of Jim's favorite childhood television shows featured puppets, including Burr Tillstrom's *Kukla, Fran, and Ollie,* and Bil Baird's puppets, Snarky Parker and Heathcliffe. Jim also enjoyed the comedy of Ernie Kovacs and the cartoon *Rocky and Bullwinkle*. He listened to radio shows like *The Green Hornet, The Shadow,* and the comedy of Stan Freberg, whose record parodies were essential to his early work. He also delighted in the performances of ventriloquist Edgar Bergen and his puppet Charlie McCarthy, who were popular in the forties. Jim loved newspaper cartoons, too, particularly those by cartoonist Ronald Searle. But one of the greatest influences on Jim was his grandmother, known to his family as "Dear." Jim and Dear shared a love for drawing and painting, and she encouraged Jim's creativity. He heeded his grandmother's advice and earned a reputation for always delivering what he promised.

would also become the foundation for his sideline poster business in college.

What really interested Jim in high school was television. Few people owned televisions in 1949, but the Henson family had a black-and-white set, with a ten-inch screen–a model typical of what was available at the time. Henson, who had hounded his parents to buy a television, loved the idea that images could be broadcast live in one location and appear at the same time in his living room. One popular TV series that he watched was Burr Tillstrom's *Kukla, Fran, and Ollie,* a family show featuring puppets. Burr operated the puppets, and his stars were Kukla, a boylike character with a round, red nose, and Ollie, a gentle dragon with a single tooth. They would talk to each other on a puppet stage and later would be joined by Fran Allison, a live actress. The three talked about everything from parties to atomic energy. It's possible that *Kukla, Fran, and Ollie* may have been the inspiration for the formation of Henson's high school puppetry club. Jim joined to help design sets, scenery, and props, even though he had no special interest in puppets at this time. One thing Jim did know, however–he wanted to find a job in television and the sooner the better.

Jim began looking for a job in television when he was sixteen, making inquiries at local stations in and around the D.C. area. His family had moved back to his mother's hometown of Hyattsville, Maryland, a suburb of Washingon, D.C., when Jim was ten, because of his father's job with the Department of Agriculture. Jim continued his search for a job in television for two years, but found nothing. Then one afternoon in his senior year of high school, two production assistants from local station WTOP visited his high school puppetry club. The station manager had sent them to find puppeteers for a Saturday morning children's program, called *The Junior Morning Show.* Jim jumped at the opportunity.

Wanting to learn more about puppetry, Henson checked out books from the library on how to make puppets. Then he rummaged through his mother's ragbag and picked out some colorful fabrics. With very basic sewing skills that he had picked up from his grandmother, who was an avid needleworker, Jim designed, cut out, and stitched together three puppets: Pierre the French Rat, based on a character he had created for a school comic strip, and two Texas cowboys, Longhorn and Shorthorn. Although Jim had little experience as a performer, he auditioned with sincerity and enthusiasm–and no doubt a good deal of natural talent. He was offered the job.

The Junior Morning Show only aired for three weeks, but out of the experience Jim got a favorable mention in a local newspaper and a chance to work in front of a television camera. Now he wanted to do more. WRC, the NBC affiliate in Washington, D.C., saw his work and the station manager found a slot for Henson's puppets on a program called *Afternoon,* a show that featured segments

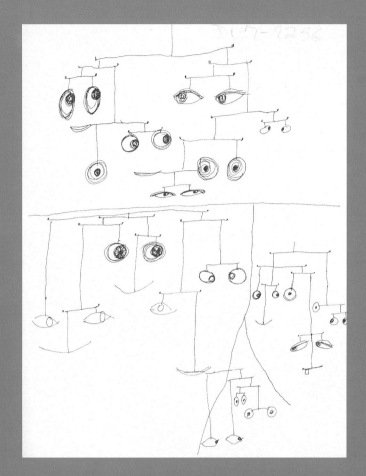

Eyes Mobiles, mobile designs. Mid 1950s. Ink, 11 x 8½"

Dot Your Eyes

In the mid-1950s American sculptor Alexander Calder popularized hanging mobiles. Calder's art had a great influence on Jim. This can be seen in a mobile of eyes and mouths that Jim drew while he was a student at the University of Maryland. The mobile presented another means for Jim to experiment artistically with facial expressions and emotions. His drawing indicates that as it rotated, the mobile would reveal constantly changing facial expressions. The eyes would shift and turn and the mouths would slip in and out of place, making different faces with each puff of air. During this period Jim also made a mobile using Ping-Pong balls—he and his brother were always fooling around with them. The original Kermit had two halves of a Ping-Pong ball for eyes.

Jim could make anything come to life—from a kitchen sponge to a chocolate layer cake—when he endowed it with a pair of eyes. He could also reveal emotions and show expression just with a character's eyes. His famous dog Rowlf has perpetually surprised eyes. Taminella Grinderfall in *Tales of the Tinkerdee,* seen in a drawing on page 56, has spiraling, hypnotic eyes that give her a bewitched expression. Some of the Muppets appear to have eyes but actually have none. Dr. Bunsen Honeydew wears glasses but has no eyes on his melon-shaped head. The Swedish Chef has such bushy eyebrows that we think of him as having eyes, although he does not.

Jim discovered that the size and placement of the pupils of the eyes greatly altered a character's expression and identity. To make a Muppet look older Jim made the pupils smaller, and for a younger look, he made the pupils larger. One pupil looking up and the other one looking down gave Cookie Monster a kooky look. Oscar the Grouch (page 106) has narrow, slightly crossed eyes that give him an intense appearance. Jim used this technique of slightly crossed eyes to make Muppets seem to be focusing on something. This made them look interested and engaged rather than empty and vacuous like some puppets.

about cooking, fashion, children, music, and news. Jim was assigned to perform puppet sketches for the children's segment.

At the same time that Jim began working at WRC, he enrolled at the University of Maryland. It was the fall of 1954. Besides television, Jim had plans to become a commercial artist. He created posters for college theater productions, campus campaigns, and a variety of student activities. One of his posters from this period was for a rock 'n' roll concert and dance, and it reflects the spirit of campus life in the mid-1950s, including a saxophone blowing colorful ribbons across the black form of a guitar.

Henson loved jazz. Since much television was performed live in the fifties, he often met entertainers at the WRC studio, many of whom were jazz musicians. Jim admired their work and soon developed a rapport with them. He learned about the attitude and language of jazz and even began collaborating on musical scores with some of the musicians. He created a hipster beat puppet named Harry, who wore dark glasses and spoke scat and jazzy nonsense syllables like *Scoop-biddly-doo-dee-baa-bing-bam!* The musicians thought Henson's puppets were very hip, and they became some of the earliest followers of the Muppets.

Jim's silkscreen piece titled *Musicians* from this same period reflects his enthusiasm for jazz. The simple cutout forms bear resemblance to his early pup-

Opposite: *Rock and Roll Concert,* poster for University of Maryland event. c. 1955–58. Silkscreen, 24 x 18"

Musicians. Mid-1950s. Tempera and collage, 9½ x 14"

ROCK
and
ROLL
CONCERT
TERPTONES
RES DICK DAVID
BELVEDE
OTHERS
AND MANY
Like with a dance after it, Man!
Richie Coliseum
May 16
8:30-10

pets, and the striking use of color shows signs of the diversity that would become the fabric of future Muppets. What Jim was trying to re-create in this silkscreen was a mood. He began all of his work by creating an alluring atmosphere or a visual landscape and then populating it with characters.

Music had always been a part of the Henson household. Jim's mother played an old pump organ that Jim and his brother, Paul, had found and repaired. When Jim was growing up, the family often gathered around the organ and sang songs from *The A. A. Milne* and *Pogo* songbooks, as well as Rodgers and Hammerstein show tunes. In the late fifties, two friends of the family, Win Nelson and Fred Dense, decided to make a record that featured organ music. Jim's mother asked Jim to design the album cover, which was playfully titled "Let's Organize!" He created an image that conveyed a mood and style typical of the fifties. The two organists look a bit like early renditions of Bunsen and Beaker from *The Muppet Show.* Jim sometimes liked to pair tall, thin characters with short, round characters. It became a way for him to visually illustrate two contrasting personalities, such as Win and Fred (pictured here), and, later, Bunsen and Beaker, and *Sesame Street's* Ernie and Bert. Even by this time, a key aspect of Henson's creativity is evident: the dynamic between contrasting shapes and personalities can be funny.

Opposite: *Beaker,* puppet design for *The Muppet Show.* 1977. Ink, 11 x 8½"

Below: *Let's Organize!* c. 1958. Record album cover, 12½ x 12½"

LIMITED EDITION RECORDS
HIGH FIDELITY

Let's ORGANIZE!

WIN NELSON
FRED DENSE
on the Hammonds

J. HENSON

Bunsen and Beaker

In 1977 Henson designed a puppet called Beaker who became the haphazard assistant of Dr. Bunsen Honeydew, chief inventor for Muppet Labs on *The Muppet Show.* Shaped like a test tube, Beaker has a large orange nose and orange hair sticking out of his head like the roots of an onion. Beaker speaks an unknown language made up solely of the words: Meep! Meep! The more fearful and panicky Beaker feels, the more high-pitched and insistent his Meep Meeps get.

Since he serves as a test dummy for Dr. Honeydew's latest inventions, Beaker lives in a perpetual state of fear. "Beaky," as Dr. Honeydew affectionately calls his sidekick, often finds himself blown up, torpedoed through walls, twisted like a pretzel, or flattened like a pancake.

To emphasize Beaker's stressful existence, Jim gave Beaker's eyes a look of permanent terror. He also designed Beaker's head to move up and down on a rod so in times of extreme fear the rod can be pulled down, making Beaker's head disappear into his collar. To show disbelief or shock, Beaker's neck can also shoot straight up like a TV antenna. The clueless, yet good-natured Dr. Honeydew remains oblivious to Beaker's fears and concerns, but the ever faithful Beaker endures the torment because deep down in his skinny, pipe-shaped soul, he believes that Dr. Honeydew will invent something truly useful—something that will make Muppet Labs famous.

Beaker

Mouth to Scream

Flesh Color
Pink Nose

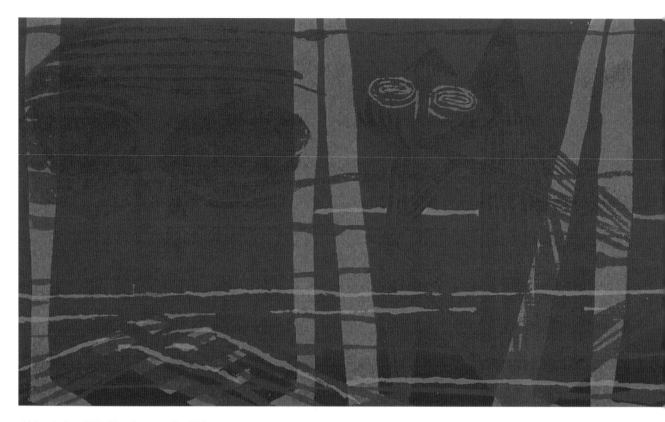

Melancholy. c. 1957–58. Silkscreen, 13 x 21″

Conceit. c. 1957–58. Silkscreen, 12 x 18″

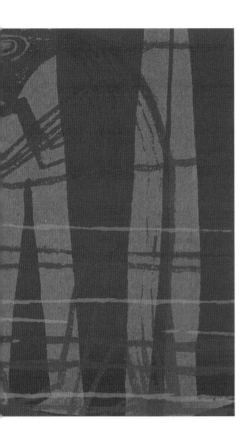

In college he designed three silkscreen prints that illustrate three facets of human personality, *Hilarity, Melancholy,* and *Conceit.* The figures in *Hilarity* are exuberant; their arms stretch upward, reaching to embrace even more laughter and exhilaration. The spirit and vitality in *Hilarity* would become the same exuberance that Kermit the Frog would express when introducing a guest star on *The Muppet Show,* waving his flippered hands and shouting, "Yaaaaaay!" This kind of contagious joy was at the heart of much of Jim Henson's work. Jim's wife, Jane, once recalled his humor this way: "[It's like] when you're in church and something doesn't happen correctly, you fall apart laughing—you can't stop." Jim gravitated toward this brand of humor, which would become the essence of Muppet humor.

In *Conceit* Jim illustrates the absurdity of self-importance. Spindly characters chip away at each others' pedestals with pickaxes. One character is even pecking at the pedestal he himself is standing on. Another has his head so far in the clouds that he's unable to see he's about to topple over. Jim's longtime friend and performing partner, Frank Oz, once said, "Jim never had his head in the clouds. He just accepted the imperfections of being human." Instead, Jim Henson loved spoofing those imperfections. Even in this early work, his characters are upstaging one another, a technique that would become a Muppet trademark. Jim Henson had a knack for separating the less attractive qualities in human nature from the good soul that he believed was a part of everyone.

In *Melancholy* the dreary characters are rendered in heavy black lines. Imprisoned by their own troubles, they are slumped inside their self-imposed confines and so can't see the legs of the living, shining all around them like rays of hope. Henson was no stranger to melancholy, but his friends have often said that he hoped his work would remind people how good life could be if they would just put things in perspective. A year before he made *Melancholy,* his older brother, Paul, was killed in a car accident. Jim rose above his sadness by concentrating on the good things in life, and pouring himself into his work. His curiosity and enthusiasm would soon lead him into unexpected new areas in both television and puppetry.

Hilarity. c. 1957–58. Silkscreen, 21 x 13"

Like the vertical figures in *Hilarity*, Jim Henson was always tall, lean, and bearded. At his mother's request, he shaved his beard for his 1959 wedding to college sweetheart and performing partner Jane Nebel. In a typical creative approach, Jim put the remains of the beard in an envelope and sent it to his fiancée with a note that said "From Samson to Delilah."

Monkipus-Chimprutipus-Orangarat, unrealized puppet designs for the Chrysler Pavilion of the New York World's Fair 1963 Marker, 14 x 11"

·•ઙ⟜ Creative Partnerships ⟞ઙ•·

After puppeteering on local television during his senior year in high school and freshman year in college, Jim was offered a job at WRC-TV in 1955. He asked Jane Nebel, a classmate from the University of Maryland, to work with him on a show called *Afternoon.* A year later, Jim was given his own evening show, *Sam and Friends,* which he performed with Jane during its remarkable six-year run.

Jim and Jane were married in 1959 and began raising a family. With the success of *Sam and Friends,* they began expanding their professional family as well. Jerry Juhl, Don Sahlin, and Frank Oz were among the earliest contributors to the Muppets–Jerry worked primarily as a writer, Don was a designer and puppet-builder, and Frank performed many of the Muppet characters.

"When it comes to the characters," explained Jerry Juhl, "it's all a collaborative effort with the writers and performers. We have a family quality that picks itself up in the writing what with all the time we spend together." Jim thrived on working collaboratively with creative and talented partners

FOAM FOLLOWS FUNCTION

"I came to puppetry more through the art side of it. Usually I would start with drawings and then turn them into puppets."

—Jim Henson

Opposite: *Kermit and Sam*, character sketch. c. 1960. Pencil, 11 x 8½"

Penciled on a piece of paper yellowed with age is the spirit of the original Kermit and Sam. Sam was the star of Jim Henson's *Sam and Friends,* a five-minute mini-variety show that aired twice nightly from 1955 to 1961. Sam had an electric expression that the drawing on page 24 doesn't fully reveal. His mouth always hung slightly open, like a dog waiting for someone to throw a ball. His ears were as big and receptive as satellite dishes and were balanced by a nose that looked like a doorknob. His eyes had a look of surprise that makes Sam appear to be in a permanent state of awe. In all, Sam was a perfect example of Jim's belief that a puppet's physical characteristics should reflect its character.

The look of wonderment on Sam's face probably reflects how Jim must have felt when he was offered the chance to do his own show. One moment "we were college students amusing ourselves," Jane recalled. And the next moment they were college students performing on prime-time television. *Sam and Friends* had two of the best time slots on television—slots that picked up a sophisticated adult audience. It came on right before the NBC evening news and again before *The Tonight Show,* then hosted by Steve Allen. Over the course of its six-year run, *Sam and Friends* would attract a large local following, and in 1958 the show won an Emmy for best local entertainment.

In this same late-fifties drawing, Kermit was not yet a frog. He was just a smiling, froglike creature who was one of Sam's friends. Jim built the original Kermit puppet from a sketch similar to this one. He then pulled an old spring coat of his mother's from her rag bag and used it for Kermit's body. He cut a Ping-Pong ball in half for the eyes.

Chicken Liver (a.k.a. *Theodore*), puppet design for *Sam and Friends.* 1959. Pencil, 8 x 17½"

With a black magic marker, he drew the pupils onto each plastic hemisphere. Although Kermit is recognizable from this drawing, he still has the crude look of an artist's early designs. His most distinct attributes—his flippers, collar, rounded body, and princely qualities—would not emerge until the late sixties when he appeared in a collection of "fractured" fairy tale productions called *Tales from Muppetland*. By this time, the "frogified" Kermit, as Jim once put it, was already his favorite character, a gentle guiding force around which all the Muppets would revolve.

Kermit played different parts on *Sam and Friends*, including Rosemary Clooney singing "I've Grown Accustomed to Your Face." All of the characters lip-synched along to popular record-

Teahouse of the August Moon. c. 1955–58. Silkscreen, 18 x 24"

ings of the day. "The early *Sam and Friends* were all record pantomimes," Jim Henson once told an interviewer. "It was a way that one could do entertaining pieces rather safely and easily, and so for years we did that and built up slightly." It also allowed him to perfect the art of lip-synching. At the time, most puppet voices often resembled old Japanese movies with dubbed-in English lines. But Henson wanted his characters to come alive on-screen, so lip-synching had to be precise. It was not a matter of just opening and closing the hand; it was more like pushing the voice from the hand so that the mouth moves precisely with the voice. One of the most important aspects of Jim Henson's work was to create the illusion that his puppets were real beings; the more he refined his puppet techniques, the more spectacular the illusions would become.

When the records began spinning, the host of *Sam and Friends* "sang" and danced frenetically to songs like Louis Prima and Keely Smith's rendition of *That Old Black Magic*. The enthusiasm that animated Sam was the same energy that buzzed inside Jim Henson. But when the cameras were switched off, Jim Henson was anything but flamboyant. His friends have often described him as soft-spoken and low-key in daily life. "There's something to hiding behind a puppet," he once said. "You're able to say things you ordinarily wouldn't say." With puppets Henson could also poke fun at politics, social mores, and the darker aspects of human nature.

In the fifties Jim sketched a design for another character, called *Carburetor Jones*. Bearing a striking resemblance to Scooter from *The Muppet Show*, Carburetor Jones was part of a group of characters that were doodled for a never-produced variety show called *The Zoocus*. The show's name was a combination of the words *zoo* and *circus*. The pencil sketch on page 28 captures the essence of Carburetor Jones—*speed*. Part of his character description was "always on motorcycle, comes roaring in, and always spins wheels when roaring off. . . . Talks mostly about motors, engines, etc."

Jim might have felt like Carburetor Jones as he tried to keep up with a demanding schedule in college and throughout his entire life. But instead of talking about engines and motors, he talked about television and puppetry. Between classes, he conceived, wrote, and rehearsed material for *Sam and Friends*, designed and built new puppets, and painted scenery and props for his show. He also worked on sets for the drama department and ran his poster business. When he had finished classes for the day, "Carburetor Jim" drove to the scene department of WRC, rehearsed his show for an hour, and performed it live at 6:25 that same evening. Then he went home to Hyattsville, grabbed a quick supper, and did some studying. At 10:30 he headed back to town for his 11:25 show. Jim would often linger for hours at the studio, listening to the producers, engineers, and technicians, trying to learn everything he could about television. "The technicians loved teaching him because he really learned his lessons well," Jane remembered. "He would tell the technicians that he'd like to try this or that, and then it would become a team thing."

Jim saw the television screen as a canvas where he could express himself as a painter, designer, sculptor, actor, and singer. The television set served as a proscenium for his puppets, and the gallery where his work appeared was the American living room. Since the television set itself served as the frame, Jim eliminated the puppet booth, thereby "freeing" the puppets to move about on TV.

To create the illusion of puppets appearing on screen like real actors, Jim and Jane kneeled in front of the cameras with their arms held high over their heads. The scenery—sometimes a city sidewalk at night with eyes peering from trash-can lids or a wooded walk with gnarled trees—would hang above and behind their heads much like a movie screen. To enable them to see their characters better, television monitors were positioned at their feet. This meant that Jim and Jane could be both performer and viewer at the same time. With the monitors they could actually see what the audience was seeing.

Carburetor Jones, puppet design for *The Zoocus* television series concept. c. 1960. Pencil, 11 x 8½ ˝

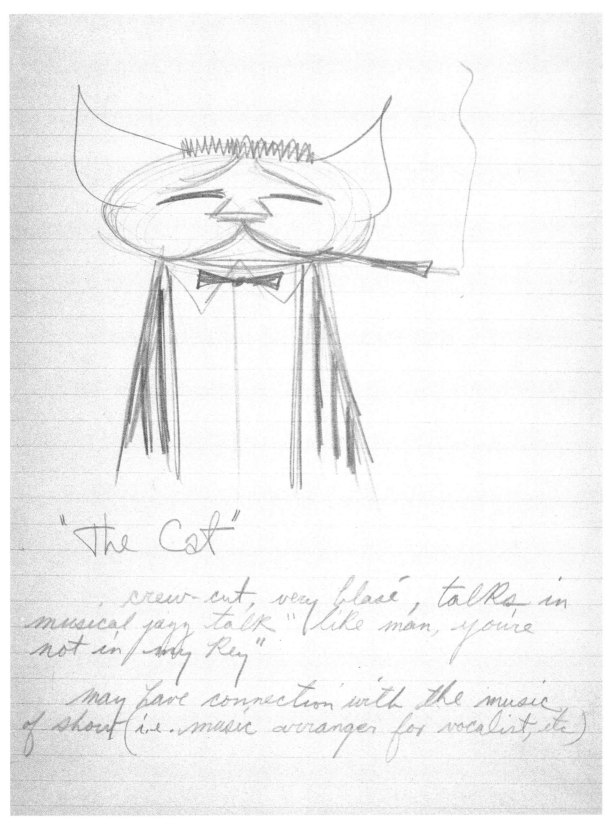

"The Cat"

, crew-cut, very blasé, talks in
musical jazz talk "like man, you're
not in my Rey"

may have connection with the music
of show (i.e. music arranger for vocalist, etc)

The Cat, puppet design for *The Zoocus* television series concept. c. 1960. Pencil, 11 x 8½"

Jim came up with the name Muppets during the *Sam and Friends* years—it is a combination of the words *marionettes* and *puppets*. The early Muppets were mostly abstract forms, neither animal nor human. "I always enjoyed doing slightly strange and surrealistic kinds of things," Jim once said. The characters had funny names—Chicken Liver, Yorick, Mushmellon, Moldy Hay, and Icky Gunk—but they possessed human personality traits, although often greatly exaggerated. Yorick, for instance, had a ravenous appetite. He ate everything in sight, including Kermit. Another character called Chicken Liver, also known as Theodore, was a dramatic storyteller who believed that *Sam and Friends* lacked culture. He promised to enrich the show with classical literature, including such epic stories as *The Three Little Pigs*.

Opposite: *Philosopher,* puppet design for *The Zoocus* television series concept. c. 1960. Pencil, 11 x 8½ "

Mr. Ripple, puppet designs for *The Zoocus* television series concept. c. 1960. Pencil, 11 x 8½ "

the Philosopher Type fellow (no name yet
acts as, oracle to whom others ask
questions & quotes quotes, usually
wrong or inappropriate, doesn't
know anything practical.

Jim began experimenting with the camera lens to manipulate depth and perspective. The studio technician would insert a wide-angle lens into the camera. Then, holding the puppet over his head, Jim would move his arm a few feet backward. This movement, together with the wide-angle lens, made the character appear to be far away. When Henson moved his arm forward a few feet, the character appeared to be close up.

In 1958, when Jim was breaking new ground in puppetry and television on *Sam and Friends,* he began to feel uncertain about his career and questioned whether or not he should continue to work with puppets for a living. He could count the number of successful puppeteers in America on one hand: Burr Tillstrom, Edgar Bergen, and Bil Baird. In the absence of a clear answer, he decided to take a break to figure things out. He left Jane and his high school friend Bob Payne in charge of *Sam and Friends,* then packed his sketchbook and went to Europe. For months he sketched, and as he traveled around Europe (including a trip to the World's Fair in Brussels) he sought out puppeteers. After learning how deeply Europeans revered the art of puppetry, Jim's perspective changed. "It was at that point I realized that puppetry was an art form, a valid way to do really interesting things. I came back from that trip all fired up to do wonderful puppetry." Jim Henson made another commitment when he returned from his trip. He and

The Zoocus, concept for a television series. c. 1960. Below: Pencil, 8½ x 11". Opposite: Pencil, 11 x 8½"

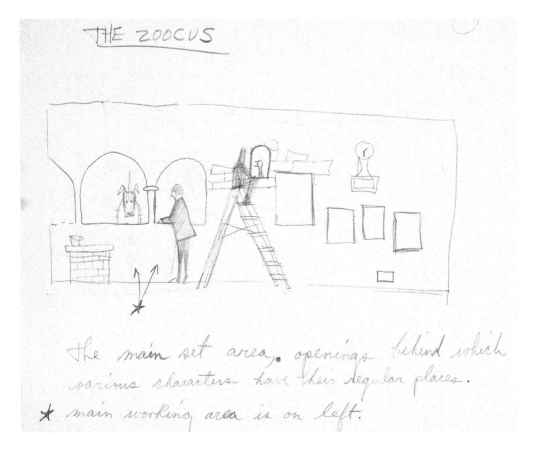

THE ZOOCUS

the main set area, openings behind which various characters have their regular places.
★ main working area is on left.

THE ZOOCUS

a foreground about 15'–20' in front of set; used as 'introduction' to show as personality walks in, etc

···❦⟨⊱—⟩ The Zoocus ⟨⊰—⟩❦···

In his pencil sketches for the *Zoocus* scenery, one of which shows an introductory set for a variety show with colonnades—an idea he would later use on *The Muppet Show*—Jim drew walls with windows where the puppets would appear. Not a conventional puppet stage, this would nonetheless be a way to hide the puppeteers as the puppets talked to guest stars. Jim would later figure out that he didn't even need to hide the puppeteers behind walls. They would simply crouch down next to the guests out of camera range so that the puppets and the guests would appear to be chatting side by side.

Jane Nebel married in 1959. After the wedding, they bought a house in Bethesda, Maryland, and turned their basement into a workshop for creating and repairing puppets for *Sam and Friends*. They now had a large family of puppets and a cat named George Washington. In 1960 they added one more member to the family, their first child, Lisa.

Jim was always adding things to Kermit—sometimes it was a yarn wig with blond braids, and other times it was a short dark-haired wig and a beaded choker. In this case Jim doodled hair and a bow with a crayon on a photograph of Kermit for an unpublished children's book called *Watermellon's I Don't Know*. The story was about Kermit, Yorick, and a cache of watermelon seeds; not knowing what to do with the discarded seeds, they let the pile grow to gargantuan proportions. Although Jim would never write another children's book, the publishing division he established in his company produces books and magazines for children based on his characters and productions. But at that time, working on local television, national variety shows, and television commercials gave him a chance to try out different ideas.

Flexible Puppets

When Jim discovered that the television screen itself could serve as a puppet theater, he did away with the traditional puppet booth. He didn't use traditional wooden puppets either. Originally, puppet shows were viewed from a certain distance, so the audience didn't notice that puppet's faces were stiff and wooden. Television brought puppets close up, and Jim wanted them to be as expressive as possible. To achieve this, he began to build puppets from soft, flexible materials. At first he experimented with fabrics found at home, along with cardboard, paint, and plastic wood. Then he discovered foam rubber, which became widely available in the 1950s. Foam rubber made a wonderful base for sculpting puppets. Once Jim formed a character's basic shape from foam, he could cover it with fleece, flocking, or feathers. Foam rubber also provided the flexibility of movement that Jim had always wanted. He could move the mouth up, down, and sideways or scrunch it up to show frustration. Not only did his puppets have the flexibility to express a range of emotions, but they were also lightweight and durable, features important to a puppeteer. When master puppet builder Don Sahlin joined Muppets, Inc., he refined Jim's puppet-building techniques and, by faithfully following Jim's drawings, helped bring the Muppets to life.

Illustration from an unpublished book, *Watermellon's I Don't Know.* 1960. Photo collage and crayon, 8¼ x 8⅜ "

"Nutty-Bird"

CARTOONS TO COMMERCIALS

"Each of us expressing our own originality is the essence of art and professionalism."

—Jim Henson

Above: Big-Eyed Monster, unrealized puppet design for the Chrysler Pavilion of the New York World's Fair. 1963. Marker, 14 x 11"

Opposite: *Nutty-Bird*, puppet design for a Royal Crown Cola advertising campaign. 1966. Watercolor and pencil, 11 x 8"

Cruising the Strip: Cartooning

Throughout the early part of his career, Jim had aspirations of becoming a cartoonist. His love of cartooning was inspired by his favorite comic strip, Walt Kelly's *Pogo,* popular in the late forties and fifties. Pogo Possum lived in the Okefenokee Swamp with his country-bumpkin friends–an alligator, a turtle, a porcupine, and others. In the days of McCarthyism, when the fear of Communism prevented Americans from speaking freely, the Pogo characters talked openly about politics. Cartooning was a safe venue to talk about issues of the day, because cartoonists could express their opinions through animals or children.

Jim recognized the power of cartoons at an early age and would later bring this same awareness to his puppets as an adult. When he was in his mid-teens he drew the cartoon on pages 40-41 (*To the Victor Belong the Spoils*) of a young boy in a suit of armor with a red cape and a feathered plume, dragging a dead dragon across a mountainous kingdom. Throughout high school, Jim entertained

"Mom, don't we need a watchdog?", unpublished cartoon. c. 1955. Ink and half-tone on cardboard, 11 x 14"

"MOM, DON'T WE NEED A WATCHDOG?"

The Watchdog

At the age of thirteen, Jim had a single-panel cartoon accepted and published by *The Christian Science Monitor.* In his teens he submitted cartoons to *The New Yorker* magazine and other publications. In "The Watchdog," one of Henson's *New Yorker*-style cartoons, the big, furry, ten-foot-tall watchdog looking for a job is a precursor to the monsters that appear frequently in his later work.

Right: Cover design for *Wildcat Scratches,* student publication from Northwestern High School. 1954. Ink on scratchboard, 9 x 6"

A smaller stick figure cat in the foreground has doodled a skull-like face with the word "Teacher" underneath on the same wall, along with a heart and the initials S.F. in the middle. The initials J.H. appear nearby, making it possible that S.F. may have been a high school crush.

Below: *Pierre the French Rat,* comic strip reprinted from the Northwestern High School student publication *Wildcat Scratches.* 1954. 9 x 12"

Talking and laughing, students roar down the hallways between classes. Smells of school lunch drift from the cafeteria. A chemistry teacher flees from his classroom, where someone has planted a stink bomb in between classes.

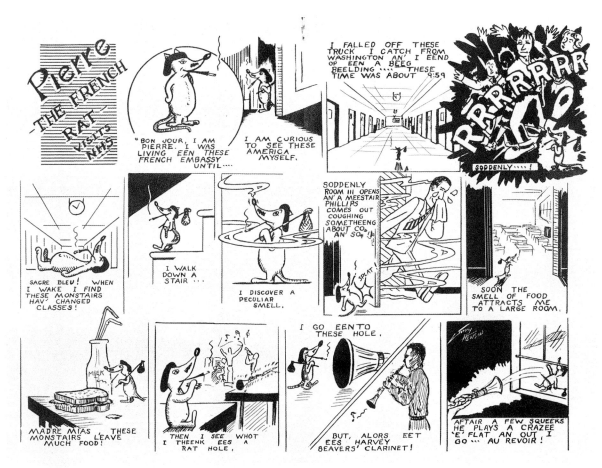

'To the victor BELONG THE Spoils'

his classmates with the cartoons he drew for school publications. On the cover of the school magazine *Wildcat Scratches,* he illustrated three feral-looking cats, painting the title onto a brick wall. The "Wildcats" were Northwestern High School's mascots.

Jim's comic strip *Pierre the French Rat* also appeared in the magazine. Through the point of view of a rat from France, Jim describes a typical American high school experience, in which students play practical jokes, make fun of school food, and have crushes on one another.

Like Walt Kelly with *Pogo,* Jim used his art to expose hypocrisy and fear, with the hope that humanity would gain some perspective. And as Jim did in most of his work, he always ended things on a humorous note. This comic strip happens to end on a "Crazee 'E' flat," when Pierre gets blown out of school from the mouth of a clarinet.

Commercial Success: The Road to Frame and Fortune

The skills Jim developed drawing cartoons became a useful foundation when he began creating storyboards for television commercials. Thanks to the success of the brief and hysterical episodes of *Sam and Friends,* in 1957 the John H. Wilkins Company approached him about creating television commercials using the Muppets to sell their coffee. This would be Jim's first foray into television advertising.

Station identifications were only eight seconds long, so Henson's commercials had to be short and to the point. Taking advantage of the adult audience he had already established, Jim often topped them with an absurd twist, such as "Use this product or you're dead." In his commercials for the Wilkins coffee company, Jim Henson created two puppets, the pickle-shaped Wilkins and his wide-mouthed, triangular sidekick, Wontkins. For Henson, who was clever with wordplay, the names Wilkins and Wontkins were variations on *will* and *won't.* Whenever Wontkins turns down a cup of Wilkins coffee, he gets shot, blown up, run over, eaten, squirted, knocked out, or clonked over the head. In one storyboard the sequence unfolds this way:

Frame 1, Wilkins: With *this* camera, I shoot pictures of people who don't drink Wilkins coffee.

Frame 2, Wontkins: I'm ready . . . shoot.

Frame 3, Wilkin's camera shoots like a cannon: BLAM!

Frame 4, Wilkins: Anybody else?

The American public loved the madness erupting from these little foam shapes. Not long after these commercials first aired, they received the highest ratings a TV commercial had ever been given. Jim's characters would die a thousand different ways, and yet the audience loved it. The real genius behind his commercials was the way Jim had cleverly summed up the public's innermost feelings about cheap sales pitches. He never made fun of a product—he made fun of commercials themselves. This was a new approach to television advertising that turned conventional advertising upside down. Up until that time, most television commercials were straightforward and unimaginative. But Henson approached selling a product through humor. The Wilkins Company liked Jim Henson's radical approach, and sales of their coffee dramatically increased. "We took a very different approach. We tried to sell things by making people laugh," Jim later said. Over time, Jim and his advertising partners would go on to make several hundred commercials for more than forty companies.

With revenue coming in from advertising, *Sam and Friends*, and guest appearances on variety shows, such as *The Arthur Godfrey Show*, *The Jack Paar Show*, *The Today Show*, and *The Will Rogers Jr. Show*, among others, Henson realized that he needed to build a team to satisfy the demand. When their second child, Cheryl, was born in 1961, Jane decided to retire from puppeteering to look after the children, and Jim began looking to hire people.

Jim and Jane traveled to California to attend the Puppeteers of America Convention. There they met Jerry Juhl, a talented puppeteer who had been working on a children's show in San Jose; he knew about the Muppets from Jim's television commercials. Jerry remembers chatting with Jim about puppetry in the parking lot one afternoon when Jim pulled a black box from the trunk of his car. "The things he brought out of that box seemed to me to be magical presences, like totems—but funnier: an angry creature whose whole body was a rounded triangle; a purple skull named Yorick; a green froglike thing. One after another, Jim pulled them from the box, put them on his hand, and brought them to life." Jerry had never seen puppets like this before. "Who is this Henson guy?" he recalled thinking. "This guy was like a sailor who had studied the compass and found that there was a fifth direction in which one could sail. When he offered me a berth on that ship, I signed on." In all, Jerry would work for the Muppets for over thirty years and would be named head writer of *The Muppet Show*. But for now he was just a new member of Muppets, Inc., which was to relocate to Manhattan in 1963.

In 1966 the Lennen & Newell Advertising Company asked Henson to design a Muppet character to sell a product called Linit Fabric Finish. This product supposedly had properties that could restore cottons and other fabrics to their original sheen. With a good dose of Muppet humor, the character had to capture "the spirit of the product" and establish brand recognition. The advertisers suggested a few ideas, such as calling the character "Linit Man," a play on Minute Man, suggesting that the product could make lifeless clothes look new at a minute's notice. This idea was discarded because the pun was too obvious. The advertiser also requested that the character wear clothing to match the design on the spray can, along with little "irons" for shoes to demonstrate how the product worked.

Jim, of course, brought his own creative and humorous abilities to the creation of the Linit character. At one point in the development process, he wrote to the advertising agency: "Here are a couple of sketches of what Linit Man might look like. In one he's sort of a parody of the White Knight [shown here], blowing his trumpet (always flat) and speaking with forsooths, odds bodkins, hey, nonny nonny, etc.

"In the other sketch [not shown], he's more like a sorcerer-type, spraying clothes and bringing them to life; maybe spraying the ironing board or clock and bringing it to life also—by mistake."

The company chose Jim's "White Knight" approach. In the ad, a downcast young woman lays a stack of clothes on her ironing board. She laments that her clothes seem dull and lifeless and wishes out loud that their original vitality could somehow be restored. When she leaves the room, a knight appears. "Behold this pile of garments!" Sir Linit exclaims. Then he tells viewers how to use Linit Fabric Finish: "Simply sprayeth and ironeth!" he says cheerily as he skates back and forth over the garments with his ironlike feet. He asks the clothes how they feel, and they jump to attention, cheering and showing their complete restoration from dullness. Victorious, Sir Linit turns to the viewer and says, "Thank thee and good day!"

Sir Linit, puppet design for a Linit Fabric Finish commercial. 1967. Marker, watercolor and pencil, 12 x 9⅛"

Top Dog!

Jim sketched two dogs in 1962, a floppy-eared hound dog named Rowlf and a small muzzled sidekick named Baskerville. Originally intended to sell Purina Dog Chow, both characters would later appear on *The Muppet Show*. Rowlf proved to be a special character for Jim. When Jim completed the first sketches for Rowlf, he did something he had never done before–he handed them over to Don Sahlin, a brilliant craftsman.

Jim had met Don at a puppet convention in Detroit. Don was there with Burr Tillstrom, creator of *Kukla, Fran, and Ollie*, for whom he built puppets. A longtime fan of the show, Jim was delighted to finally meet Burr. Two years later, in 1962, Jim asked Don to come to Washington, D.C., to help him build Rowlf. Somehow Don captured the exact personality and character of Rowlf simply by referring to one of Jim's drawings. Astonished by the results, Jim invited Don to work for Muppets, Inc., and the two of them worked together for seventeen years until Don passed away in 1978.

Opposite: *Baskerville*, puppet design for a Canadian Purina Dog Chow commercial. 1962. Pencil, 11 x 8½"

Below: *Rowlf and Baskerville*, puppet designs for a Canadian Purina Dog Chow commercial. 1962. Pencil, 17 x 22"

Puppet design for a Canadian
Purina Dog Chow commercial,
1962. Pencil, 11 x 8½"

Rowlf, puppet design for a Canadian
Purina Dog Chow commercial, 1962.
Pencil, 11 x 8½"

For Henson, Don's real gift was an ability to intuit and reproduce a character from one of his sketches. "I would generally do a little scribble on a scrap of paper–which Don would regard with a certain reverence as being the 'essence' which he was working toward. Don had a very simple way of working–reducing all nonessential things and honing in on what was important. [He] had more to do with the basic Muppet style that people think of as 'the Muppets' than anybody else." Don streamlined the characters to make them look as if they had the same origin and were of a similar species. He once dubbed himself "The Guardian of the Essence," according to principal Muppet puppeteer and veteran puppet builder Dave Goelz. Don would not let a puppet out of the workshop unless it had a clearly defined look and personality, the "essence" of the character.

Don also invented "The Magic Triangle," which refers to the area between the focal point of the eyes in relation to the nose and mouth. Don thought that the eyes had to be positioned in exactly the right way, otherwise the character wouldn't come to life. "Don paid particular attention to the placement of the eyes because that single decision seemed to finalize the character more than anything else," Jim once said. "It would be the last thing he would do, and he always wanted me there, to make sure it was right for both of us–making sure the eyes had a point of focus, because without that you had no character." Jim approved of any invention that would make a character appear more believable. He wanted the audience to forget the characters were puppets. And they often did. Sometimes the cue card holder would even forget and hold up the cue cards for Rowlf!

Practical Jokers

Funny and outlandish things frequently happen at The Jim Henson Company, especially in The Muppet Workshop. Stocked with fabrics, feathers, baubles, and tools, it has always been a haven for practical jokes. Don Sahlin was the king of Muppet pranksters. One joke he liked to play involved making a dressmaker's mannequin into a monster. He would rig the monster with pulleys and ropes in the workshop's bathroom so that it would jump out when an unsuspecting worker opened the door. Don was also known to produce a skittering mouse. A little gray piece of fur fabric wrapped around a metal bolt with a piece of yarn for the tail formed the mouse's body. Don lightly tacked the "mouse" to the floor with a hatpin. Then he attached a reel with a thousand feet of rubber band to the mouse, winding the rubber band around the legs of tables and stools throughout the workshop and back to his desk. When he triggered a special mechanism, the mouse would scurry around everyone's feet, sending the squeamish ones off like rockets. Another time he tripped a switch that dumped five hundred Ping-Pong balls on Jerry Juhl's head when he sat down at his desk one morning. A master of special effects, Don once created a minor explosion that blew up the desk of principal puppeteer Dave Goelz. Sahlin would go to any length for a good scare.

Marketing the Muppets

As the Muppets became popular, Henson began to license some of his characters. In 1966 Ideal Toys produced plush versions of some of the early characters, including Rowlf, Kermit, and the Snerfs. (The Snerfs were monster puppets whose necks moved up and down on rods. Their feet were the puppeteer's hand fitted inside a furry glove at the base of the neck.) Jim drew a story-board for a television commercial for Ideal Toys in which the tongue-in-cheek sales pitch included lines like, "So buy us at once, we're a bundle of charms, and if you don't buy us, we'll break both your arms."

Henson's early licensing efforts were simply ways to support his growing business and growing family. When *Sesame Street* became popular, however, Jim changed his approach to merchandising. It didn't seem right for his characters to appear on an educational show like *Sesame Street* and be used to sell commercial products on the side. "You develop a sense of responsibility," Jim once said. "You realize the importance of what you're putting out there to young kids." When *Sesame Street* began earning praise from educators, Jim raised his standards when it came to all aspects of merchandising his charac-ters. He refused to permit them to be used to sell, advertise, or market other products, and when the characters were repro-duced as toys they had to be safe for children and made of first quality materials. The Jim Henson Company still tries to adhere to these high standards in all their licensing endeavors.

Left and below: From the sto-ryboard for an Ideal Toys com-mercial featuring Kermit, Rowlf, and Snerf dolls. 1966. Pencil and ink, 23½ x 19" (full page)

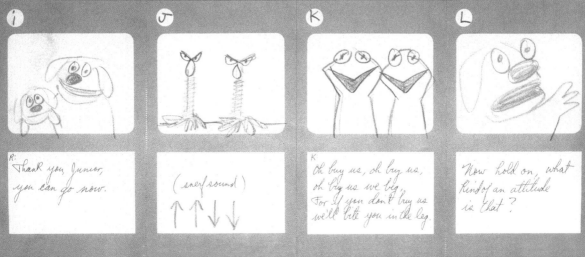

R: Thank you, Junior, you can go now.

(snerf sound)
↑ ↑ ↑ ↓ ↓ ↓

K: Oh buy us, oh buy us, oh buy us we beg, For if you don't buy us we'll bite you in the leg.

Now hold on, what kind of an attitude is that?

After Rowlf made his dog food commercial, he was stored in a cupboard until Jim pulled him out a year later. He needed a character to perform on *The Jimmy Dean Show*. From 1963 until 1966, Rowlf and Jimmy Dean chatted about anything from vaudeville to politics—to Rowlf's love interest, Lassie. Rowlf, with his wonderful dry sense of humor, often upstaged Jimmy Dean with clever come-backs and witty asides. At the end of their conversations Jimmy and Rowlf almost always sang a duet. Every week Jim would work with the show's writers to perfect Rowlf's sketch. These veteran comedy writers taught Jim about setting up a joke and delivering a punch line. This training would provide Jim with a solid foundation for his comedy sketches on *The Muppet Show*.

Before Rowlf was created, Jim worked mostly with hand-and-rod puppets. Rowlf was a "live-hand" puppet. That meant it took two puppeteers to operate him, one to control the head and the left hand, and one to control the right hand. Jim hired Frank Oz, a talented nineteen-year-old who was eager to learn, to operate the right hand. Frank went on to perform such memorable characters as Bert, Fozzie Bear, Grover, Miss Piggy, and Animal. With Frank, Jerry, and Don on board, Jim and Muppets, Inc., were on the road to success.

Sour Bird, puppet design for a Royal Crown Cola advertising campaign. 1966. Watercolor and pencil, 11 x 8"

real fingers inside octavo

"Sour-Bird"

Wake-up Call: The La Choy Dragon

The La Choy Dragon was the first full-costume puppet that Henson created. Very similar in color to this water-color-and-marker drawing, the large tangerine-colored dragon with purple and dark orange scales wore a little chef's hat on top of his head instead of horns. (Henson loved the hot colors of felt-tip marker pens.) Don gave the La Choy Dragon's features a softer, more Muppety look when he built the puppet. The legs were made so that a puppeteer could slip them on like a pair of heavy socks, only these socks had webbed feet made of foam.

When the final take for the La Choy Chow Mein commercial was shot, it was about three o'clock in the morning. Jim, Frank, and Don were feeling a little punchy, and they thought it would be funny to wake up their friend and colleague Jerry Juhl and play it back to him. This is what he heard coming through his telephone that night:

The La Choy Dragon, puppet design for a series of commercials for La Choy food products. 1966. Marker, pencil, and gouache, 11¾ x 12¾"

Lady: What do you feed twelve hungry boy scouts?

La Choy Dragon bellows: May I make a suggestion?

Lady (frightened): Who are you?

La Choy Dragon (loudly): I'm La Choy Dragon!

Boy Scout: Wow! A real dragon!

La Choy Dragon (matter-of-factly): What you need is La Choy Chow Mein.

(Sound effects: Cans crashing from shelves.)

La Choy: It's never mushy. It's crisp and crunchy.

Lady (sincerely): It is, huh?

La Choy Dragon: It's quick-cooked by me in dragon fire!
     (Sound effects of dragon breath: Haaaaa!) Quick
     cooking makes it as crisp as the take-out kind.

(Sound effects: Crackling sounds of fire as the labels and display
     sign go up in flames; spraying sound as a grocer puts it out.)

La Choy Dragon (bellowing): And one more thing! Try La Choy Noodles!

(Sound effects: More cans crash to the floor.)

La Choy Dragon: A perfect meal in six minutes. Buy some today!

(Sound effects: Sound of many cans crashing to the floor as La Choy
     Dragon walks away, swishing his tail.)

Lady, earnestly: I will! I will!

TV Announcer: La Choy Chow Mein tastes better than the
     take-out kind, 'cause it's quick-cooked in dragon fire.

(Sound effects: Crackling fire of can labels on fire.)

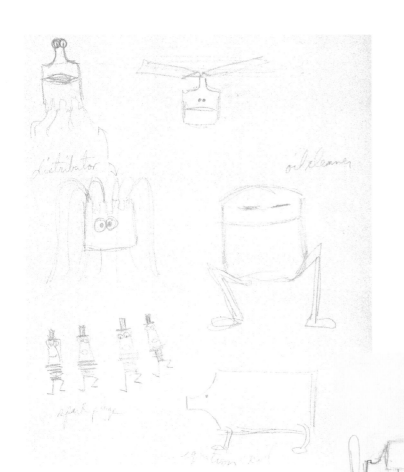

Opposite: *Charlie*, puppet design for an American Standard Oil Company commercial. 1966. Pencil and gouache, 12 x 9″

Below: *Clyde*, puppet design for an American Standard Oil Company commercial. 1966. Pencil and gouache, 12 x 9″

Above: *Engine Part Puppets*, unrealized puppet designs for the Chrysler Pavilion of the New York World's Fair. 1963. Pencil, 9½ x 8½″

Left: *Charlie*, puppet design for an American Standard Oil Company commercial. 1966. Pencil and gouache, 12 x 9″

SPINNING MUPPET TALES:

From Storyboards to Storytelling

"One of the things that I like to
do most is to break new ground."

—Jim Henson

Opposite: *Taminella Grinderfall,* puppet design for a television
pilot, *Tales of The Tinkerdee.* 1962. Pencil, 24 x 18"

$Shortly$ after Henson returned from Europe in 1958, he wrote an original script and sketched sets for a production of *Hansel and Gretel,* inspired, probably, by images of traditional folk and fairy tales and the beautifully crafted puppets that he had seen in Europe. In his retelling of *Hansel and Gretel,* Jim sticks closely to the original story, though his lighthearted sense of humor occasionally filters through the narrative. At one point, when the woodcutter and his wife bring the children to the woods with the intention of abandoning them, the woodcutter mistakes this unhappy occasion for a family outing. "We ought to go on picnics more often!" he exclaims. In retelling this well-known tale, Jim begins to learn how to craft a story. Until this time his focus had been on simple pantomimes, short comedy sketches, and television commercials. By studying and retelling traditional folk and fairy tales, Henson became more interested in exploring the basics of story structure and theme. He enjoyed tackling subjects that involved good and evil, arrogance and greed, weakness and courage, all woven into journeys through fantastic worlds.

Some of Jim's set drawings for *Hansel and Gretel* still exist today. They show thorny vines with mischievous eyes, a gnarled tree and a jagged tree stump with ghostly faces. Here the trees are reminiscent of the ill-tempered apple trees in *The Wizard of Oz,* one of Jim's favorite movies. Jim infused life into almost anything he drew—trees, plants, vegetables, animals, and inanimate objects. The flora and fauna in his later work developed more personality and became more fantastic as time went on with tentacled vines, menacing crablike creatures, and bogs of eternal stench.

The worlds of fantasy and magic suited Henson's imagination. The woods in his landscape drawing for *Hansel and Gretel* are filled with mist, dark and alive with danger. Yet no matter how dangerous or confusing the setting might be, Jim always included a glimmer of hope for the main character. Sometimes this took on the form of a sign, a symbol, or a kind and helpful character. A note in the corner of this drawing reads, "rather dark, but when lit bright, can be cheerful." This seemingly nonchalant phrase underlies much of Jim's darker works. He always wanted his characters to be able to find their way out of a predicament. Here, Jim is consciously thinking of possibilities for the protagonist to find his or her way to safety.

Although this version of *Hansel and Gretel* was never produced, in 1965 Jim used a whimsical take-off on the story to sell a product. He created a commercial storyboard for two miracle products called Pak Nit and Pak Nit RX. This was at a

Set design for a puppet performance of *Hansel and Gretel.* 1959. Pencil, 14 x 17″

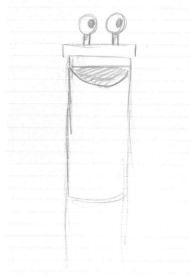

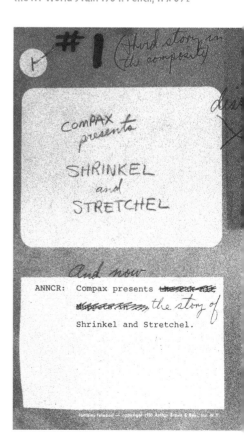

time before there were such products as dryer sheets to prevent clothes from wrinkling. These new products claimed to prevent clothes from shrinking, stretching, or wrinkling in the dryer. In this brief retelling, the children who are trying to find their way through the woods are named Shrinkel and Stretchel. In their wanderings they come across a gingerbread house, inhabited by a witch with spiraling hypnotic eyes, a fang, razor stubble, and a cackling voice. Within moments of meeting the children, the witch hurls them into her oven. But at the sound of a timer, Shrinkel and Stretchel pop out of the oven, starched, pressed, and smiling. The witch is amazed by how well their clothing has held up under such extreme heat. Shrinkel and Stretchel explain the virtues of Pak Nit and Pak Nit RX: shrinkage control and shape control. The witch is so delighted by this discovery that she sheds her wicked veneer, along with her appetite for children, for a new and improved image–or at least a presentable wardrobe. Often Henson recycled characters, adapting them to various milieus. The witch, for example, was used later in the television special *The Frog Prince,* and some of the characters in the laundry commercial were originally created for *Tales of the Tinkerdee,* a 1962 television pilot.

Jim Henson "fractured" the original story of *Hansel and Gretel* in this commercial, taking the opposite approach to his first retelling of this story six years earlier. The storyboards he used to create advertisements also helped him to tell a story sequentially, frame by frame. He also produced and directed most of his own commercials. With a talented team of co-workers to help him with the television commercials and variety shows, Jim devoted more time and energy developing his interest in filmmaking. It was only a matter of time until he would begin to combine storytelling with filmmaking.

When Henson was in college, he bought a 16-millimeter Bolex camera and an animation stand and began to make animated films. First he animated his own artwork. "I started painting on a sheet of paper placed under the lens on the bed of the animation stand," he told an interviewer. "I would just paint a couple of strokes and take a frame or two of film, and I would be able to watch this painting evolve and move." After college, Henson experimented further with animation and he also began to make home movies. From 1964 to 1968, he used storyboards to create longer narratives and produced a series of short film montages. "I used to think in terms of having two careers," he once recalled. "One was accepted by the audience and successful, and this was the Muppets. And the other, filmmaking, was something that I was very interested in and enjoyed very much despite the fact that it didn't have commercial success." His most acclaimed short film was an 8½-minute montage entitled *Time Piece*, which combined animation and real actors and used only visual images to tell this story.

Jim made several other short films in the mid-sixties, including *Youth '68,*

Shrinkel and Stretchel, storyboard for a Pak Nit commercial. 1965. Pencil, 8¼ x 18½"

which reflected the generation gap of the sixties, and *The Cube,* a surrealistic fable of a man who thinks he is trapped inside a cube. Both were produced for *Experiment in Television,* an hour-long show on NBC that showcased young talent. But *Time Piece* proved to be his greatest effort of this period.

The film is about a man imprisoned by time and running away from time. It unfolds in a stream of images, accompanied by a soundtrack that resembles what time might sound like if it could be heard: ticking clocks, racing bongo beats, horses galloping, the pounding of a judge's gavel, bells ringing, the gurgling of a drain. Interspersed between these images is a man, played by Jim, running through a city, across a countryside, through a cemetery, flying through the air with wings, all the while stopping to engage in odd activities such as painting an elephant pink or shooting the *Mona Lisa* in the eye with a pistol. The film was nominated for an Academy Award in 1965. But the real triumph for Jim in his experimental film projects was learning how to combine powerful visual imagery, together with music, to tell a story. He would pursue this technique with great success in his later work, but first he would practice telling stories by using straightforward narratives.

During the sixties, the Muppets were making regular appearances on *The Ed Sullivan Show, The Today Show,* and all the other prime-time television variety shows. Despite the Muppets' popularity, Jim was unable to convince the networks that they should have a show of their own–something he earnestly desired. He held on to the idea of a show featuring the Muppets and began to give more

garment
made
skin

up
so!?

elvows
go up →

King Goshposh (opposite) and
Taminella Grinderfall (this page),
character drawings from a
sketchbook. 1962. Ink, 8½ x 5½"

thought to character development. Except for Rowlf, who was developed over a three-year period on *The Jimmy Dean Show*, the Muppet characters were not appearing regularly. Jim needed the opportunity to create fully developed, well-rounded characters. From 1968 until 1972, he created that opportunity for himself by producing a series of one-hour TV specials called *Tales from Muppetland*. The idea was to use the Muppets and their particular brand of humor to spoof well-known fairy tales. These included *Hey, Cinderella!*, *The Frog Prince*, and *The Muppet Musicians of Bremen*.

Three of the drawings for the cast of *Hey, Cinderella!* still survive today in one of Jim's early sketchbooks. In one rendering, King Goshposh, a greedy, cigar-chomping Texan who bears a resemblance to *The Ugly American*, rules over a comical nonsense kingdom. In most scenes, a trickle of real smoke streams from the end of his cigar, which is permanently attached to the corner of his mouth. His crown fits like a ring over his cone-shaped head. Bedecked in colorful robes of purple and red to match his crown and staff, King Goshposh is as pompous and self-serving as he is harmless and amusing. The king is also prone to making puns. To develop this character, Jim gave him a heavy Southern accent and added such characteristics as the smoking cigar and an exaggerated love of getting presents.

In another drawing, the king's attendant, Featherstone, is shaped like a long, thin triangle with two eyes perched on top of his pointy head. Another tri-

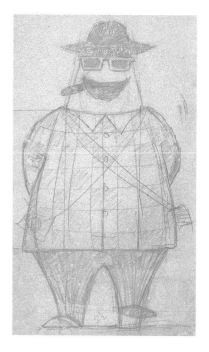

The Ugly American, animatronic puppet design for a USIA exhibit. c. 1961. Pencil, 25¼ x 14½"

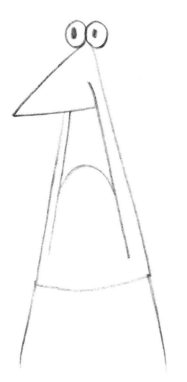

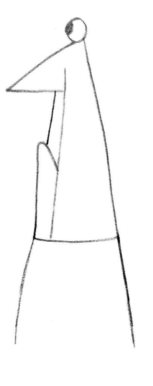

Left: *Featherstone*, puppet design for a television pilot, *Hey Cinderella!* 1965. Pencil, 12 x 9"

Opposite: *Splurge*, puppet design for a television pilot, *Hey Cinderella!* 1965. Pencil, 12 x 9"

SPLURGE

Opposite: *Taminella Grinderfall,*
character drawing from a
sketchbook. 1962. Ink, 8½ x 5½"

angle forms his nose, and his downturned mouth opens like a castle drawbridge when he speaks. Featherstone has the personality and accent of a long-suffering English butler who must continually endure the king's harebrained logic. Jim puts King Goshposh and Featherstone in the story of *Cinderella,* which is both unexpectedly funny and original. (In his later work, Jim's characters are more complex with more evident needs, desires, and motivations.)

The third drawing for *Hey, Cinderella!* shows an imposing monster with shaggy blue fur named Splurge. One of Henson's first full-costume puppet characters, Splurge stood eight feet tall and played a sidekick to Taminella Grinderfall, a witch. Splurge has two unique characteristics: a fetish for radishes and a deep voice that sounds like a 45 record played at 33 rpm. (In the story, he finds Cinderella's missing glass slipper buried in his radish patch. Splurge's fondness for radishes is re-employed in *Fraggle Rock,* in which the Fraggles love radishes.) Later Jim would create more sophisticated full-costume monsters that were operated by cable controls and mechanical devices; this allowed for more naturalistic facial emotions, dexterity, and movement.

Taminella Grinderfall was Henson's first villainess. She made her debut in his sketchbook, alongside King Goshposh, and then appeared later in a more detailed pencil drawing. Both characters were drawn in 1962 for a television pilot called *The Tales of the Tinkerdee.* Although the tales were never produced,

Incognito: Masks and Masquerade Balls

With puppets, Henson could say and do things that he might not normally have said or done in person. Jim liked masquerade balls for some of the same reasons; being incognito allowed him to be as foolish, strange, or outspoken as he wanted to be. Some of his television and movie productions–*Hey, Cinderella!* in 1970 and *Labyrinth* in 1986, among others–included masquerade balls.

In *Hey, Cinderella!* King Goshposh, played by Jim, declares that he is going to hold a masquerade ball to help find a bride for the Prince. Dubious of his father's scheme, the Prince declares that he might not recognize the right girl if everyone was wearing a mask. Jovially slapping his firstborn son on the back, the comical king assures the Prince that wearing a mask is "a great icebreaker!" *Labyrinth,* hosted by David Bowie (who plays a Goblin King) features a dreamlike ball showing guests in lavish costumes.

But it wasn't only in his productions that Henson liked masquerade balls. In 1984, he hosted his first masquerade ball for his company. It was his way to celebrate the collective talent of the people who worked for him. The locations changed from year to year, but twice Henson workers showed up at New York City's Waldorf-Astoria Hotel dressed as unusual birds, speckled birch trees, cooked lobsters, and four-eyed freaks. Jim loved the wild inventiveness of their costumes, and often employees would make him guess who might be behind their masks.

Taminella, also known as Tammy, appeared as the witch in the Pak Nit Shrinkel and Stretchel commercial. She also posed as the king's sister in *The Frog Prince* and as the villainess in *The Great Santa Claus Switch,* a Christmas special that first aired on television in 1970. Although Jim's sketchbook drawing of Taminella features her fang, hag hair, and bewitching smile, she hasn't fully evolved into the deranged character she later becomes. Taminella and the Frackles were forerunners to Jim's truly villainous characters, such as the Skeksis in his 1982 film, *The Dark Crystal.* These evil creatures looked something like the "green bird" Frackle pictured in Jim's 1970 drawing. The Skeksis looked more sinister and vulturelike and were as large and mobile as humans. Dressed in richly decorated robes, they were known to drink "the living essence" of their prey. In comparison to his later villains, Taminella and the Frackles seem pretty harmless.

Jim developed into a storyteller with a vivid sense of how images, sound, and special effects could move a story. He created worlds where goodness is won in the midst of darkness and doubt. Jim always provided hope for his characters just as he expressed it in the margins for his *Hansel and Gretel* set design: "rather dark, but when lit bright, can be cheerful."

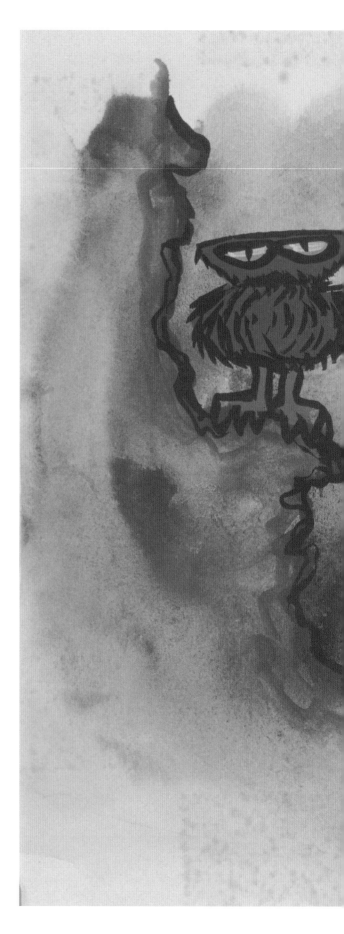

Some More Frackles, illustration for a proposal for the television special *The Sinister Santa Claus Switch.* c. 1967. Watercolor, 11 x 8½"

SOME MORE
FRACKLES

Frackles, puppet designs for the television special *The Great Santa Claus Switch.* 1970. Ink and marker, 9 x 12"

A *Group of Frackles*, illustration for a proposal for
the television special *The Sinister Santa Claus Switch*.
c. 1967. Watercolor, 11 x 8½"

A GROUP OF FRACKLES

Rockettes, illustration for a proposal for the television special *The Sinister Santa Claus Switch*. c. 1967.
Watercolor, 11 x 8½"

DANCE NUMBER DONE BY THE ELVES
DISGUISED AS ROCKS [THE ROCKETTES?]

···❧ ⟨ Little Shop of Creatures ⟩ ···

For a 1970 Christmas special, *The Great Santa Claus Switch*, produced by Ed Sullivan's company, Jim invented a new species of characters called the Frackles. The story revolved around an evil magician's failed plot to kidnap and impersonate Santa Claus in order to rob every home in the world. The Frackles–with names like Growl, Mutter, Snarl, Scoff, Snicker, and Gloat–were this wicked magician's henchmen. The Great Gonzo is probably the best known of the species. (Rather than working from a sketch, Jim carved him directly out of foam.) Before he became the weird and lovable Gonzo, he was the Cigar Box Frackle.

These early drawings influenced the artistic direction of a later evil species, known as the Skeksis, designed by Brian Froud for Henson's 1982 fantasy film *The Dark Crystal*. More elaborate and complex than anything Jim had ever created, these mechanized or "animatronic" puppets were produced at his London workshop, The Creature Shop. The designers and builders there shared Jim's love of trying to create the illusion that such fantastical creatures actually live and breathe. "Working as I do with the movement of puppet creatures," Jim once said, "I'm always struck by the feebleness of our efforts to achieve naturalistic movement. Just looking at the incredible movement of a lizard or a bird, or even the smallest insect, can be a very humbling experience."

Snake Frackle, character sketch for *The Great Santa Claus Switch*. 1970. Pencil and marker, 8 x 5"

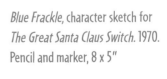

Dripsnout Frackle, character sketch for *The Great Santa Claus Switch*. 1970. Pencil and marker, 8 x 5"

Blue Frackle, character sketch for *The Great Santa Claus Switch*. 1970. Pencil and marker, 8 x 5"

Blue Frackle, character sketch for *The Great Santa Claus Switch*. 1970. Pencil and marker, 8 x 5"

tap dancing
singing
unicycle
juggling
playing instruments - piano - trumpet
comedy sketches
drummer - on top
can can girl
orchestra pit talent

LAUGH TRACKS:

Comedy Sketches for Variety Shows

"Puppets are fortunate—they can do and say things a live performer wouldn't touch with a stick."

—From a 1969 Proposal for *The Muppet Show*

Above: *Long-tailed Monster*, puppet design. Late 1960s. Pencil, 11 x 8½"
Opposite: *The Entertainers*, television concept. Late 1960s. Pencil, 11 x 8½"

$Jump~On$ the bandwagon! With cameras rolling, a group of top-hatted entertainers have boarded a kind of circus wagon. Tipping their hats and tooting their horns, they roll along toward their next act. This cheery spectacle is a doodle from Jim Henson's late 1960s idea file. Jim's handwritten notes at the top of the page indicate that The Entertainers sing, tap dance, juggle, ride a unicycle, play musical instruments, and perform comedy sketches. There is even a high-kicking can-can girl on board.

This vaudevillian party on wheels illustrates Jim's vision for a variety show that featured the Muppets. Their first incarnation was in a Valentine's Day special in 1973 and a pilot in 1975. But the gang didn't appear in their own television show, or in this particular form, until 1976. Prior to this, guest appearances on variety shows throughout the sixties and early seventies provided Jim and his merry band of puppeteers with opportunities to refine comedy pieces and perfect musical numbers. As the Muppets' popularity grew, the offers for guest appearances had the phone ringing off the hook at Muppets, Inc.

Al Hirt, variety show idea. 1965. Pencil on paper, 11 x 8½"

Most comedy routines poke fun at the mundane events of everyday life, and this is what Jim Henson's Muppets did best of all. The more Jim indulged in exaggeration and absurdity in his performances, the more he enabled his audience to look at themselves humorously and put their foibles in perspective. Most of all, Jim Henson wanted to remind people to have fun and to see the good in life.

Jim created a hairy hippie creature called Mahna-Mahna for a comedy sketch he performed in 1970 on *The Ed Sullivan Show*. Mahna-Mahna, who was named after a popular song recorded by Italian artist Umilioni that accompanied the skit, was the epitome of freedom from inhibitions. In Jim's drawing the character appears to have huge, fully dilated eyes. The puppet's eyes were made from soft foam rings with yellow rims. His electrified hairdo and beard became bright orange. The squiggly lines that outlined his body became a furry green vest. The drawing also featured two shocking pink cowlike creatures that were called "Snouths," a blend of the words *snout* and *mouth*. The Snouths had false eyelashes and their bodies were covered with pink shag fabric. As the catchy tune plays, the hippie blurts out his name, Mahna-Mahna, to which the Snouths joyously respond "Doo Doo Dee Doo-Doo!" As the sketch progresses, Mahna-Mahna gets carried away by the song. He is so happy singing that the

Mahna-Mahna, puppet design for variety show appearances. Late 1960s. Ink, 8¾ x 5⅞"

Snouths stop their refrain and watch him in disbelief. The music pauses too, except for the beat, and Mahna-Mahna gives an innocent look as if to say, *What?* When the music starts again, he loses himself in the song. Before long he completely upstages the Snouths. Jim Henson had this same uncontainable enthusiasm for life. In Mahna-Mahna he celebrates the freedom and joy of self-expression, a concept that had become newly popular in the sixties.

Jim's comedy sketches often combined bizarre and sometimes shocking visual images that demanded the attention of the audience. Many of his pieces were parables about power and powerlessness. His love of jazz often played a part in these sketches, too. Characters conversed in rhythmical nonsense terms as in a piece called *Sclrap Flyapp*. In the early sixties, Henson drew several bizarre creatures for this sketch that were first featured on *The Today Show* and later on *The Tonight Show*. The characters had pipe-shaped bodies, no arms, and mythical totem heads with horrified expressions on their faces. Filmed in black-and-white, three of the creatures inhabited a smoke-filled landscape. One at a time, they

"When you can't think of an ending, go out with a bang!"

—The Wizard from the *Wizard of Id* as performed by Jim Henson

NBC Pipes

One day in 1964, the Muppets were scheduled for a 10:00 A.M. guest appearance on *The Jack Paar Show* at NBC studios in Rockefeller Center. Filming fell behind schedule and they were asked to wait. Cooped up in a dressing room all day, Jerry Juhl, Frank Oz, Don Sahlin, and Jim began to get restless. At one point, one of them opened a door in the room to see where it went. It turned out to be a utility closet, housing a network of pipes of different sizes and shapes, with thick metal joints, cranks, washers, bolts, and faucets.

Jim looked at the pipes and saw an opportunity to relieve their boredom. Using the paints that Don had brought to touch up characters, they began to paint Muppet faces on the pipes. "It was a typical Jim idea," Jerry Juhl recalled. "As the whole thing got more elaborate, one of us hopped into a cab and brought over more material from the workshop." They decorated the pipes with an array of grimacing faces with crossed eyes, as well as ferocious faces with protruding metal nozzles for noses. One face wore a pair of plastic sunglasses, and several others had fake hair on top of their heads. The entire labyrinth of pipes was covered with eyes, faces, designs, and flowers. "People at NBC began to hear about the crazy closet and stopped by, asking if they could take pictures," Jerry Juhl said. "At some point, late in the afternoon, there was a knock on the door and a voice outside said, 'Hello, I'm Charlton Heston. Could I see your closet?' Since practical jokes weren't unknown in our world, we yelled back, 'Yeah, sure, you're Charlton Heston.' And of course, it was Charlton Heston."

This Muppetized closet, a prime example of Jim and his team's boundless creative impulse, still exists today in the NBC building.

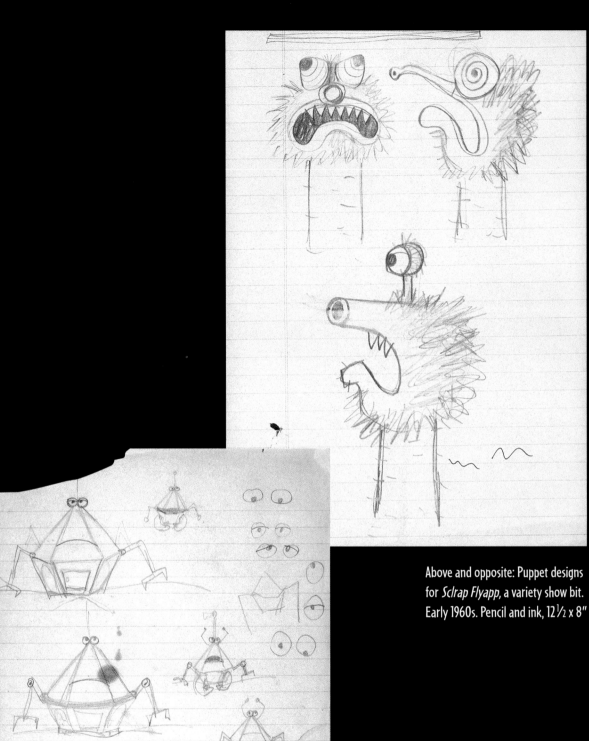

Above and opposite: Puppet designs for *Sclrap Flyapp,* a variety show bit. Early 1960s. Pencil and ink, 12½ x 8"

Left: *Martian Landing,* variety or live show idea sketch. Late 1960s. Pencil, 11 x 8½"

Buggy Mugger, sketch for Nancy Sinatra's Las Vegas show. 1971. Ink and pencil, 9 x 12"

popped up into the swirling smoke. A sneaky guitar line, like someone tiptoeing around in the dark, accompanies the sketch, and a snare drum adds to the eerie mood. In all of his comedy pieces, Jim Henson experimented with music, visual imagery, and special effects. Here he has created a spooky landscape and populated it with surrealistic creatures that speak nonsense alongside a jazz riff. Throughout the sixties and into the seventies, Jim worked on perfecting different versions of *Sclrap Flyapp.* A 1971 drawing called *Buggy Mugger* was Jim's most finished version of this piece. This time, instead of repeating *Sclrap Flyapp,* the characters converse by saying *Huggy Wuggy Buggy Muggers.* Each time, the smallest and seemingly most innocent creature enters, challenges the big guy and wins.

Jim Henson's irreverence was always something the whole family could enjoy. In 1965 he sketched a spunky group of reindeer for a comedy bit that appeared on the *Perry Como Christmas Special.* In his drawing Jim shows the reindeers' bodies, but in the final creation he pares them down to the simplest form, showing them only from the neck up. Had he given them cumbersome bodies, they wouldn't have been able to perform the visual comedy that made this sketch so delightful. "How the characters play a particular moment on a punch line is very visual," Henson said. "These are not just characters up there telling jokes. The humor only holds if there's an interaction between the characters that is visual at the same time." When Charlie calls his spirited reindeer team to attention, they instantly cluster together. With one swift movement, the reindeer become a mass of kooky eyes and intertwined antlers, standing at attention. (He even made sure each set of antlers was distinct from the others.) Their ability to come together quickly was the visual gag in this routine, and the jokes often revolved around their antlers—one reindeer jokes that he's "gonna get a job as a hat rack." Charlie, played by Jim, always has to settle this boisterous herd of reindeer, and in a Humphrey Bogart accent he often refers to them

Reindeer, puppet design for
Perry Como's Christmas show.
1965. Ink, 10⅛ x 8¼"

as "branch brains" and "twig heads." In the final lineup, the reindeer looked much like the group at the top of the picture.

In a comedy bit known as *Java*, performed to Al Hirt's song from the 1960s and designed by Frank Oz, two pieces of what looks like vacuum cleaner hose, each arched like a Slinky, perform on top of a flat surface. The bigger hose's eyes look to one side suspiciously. The small hose has wide, innocent eyes with a hint of mischief. Both have a ring of brightly colored fur around each of their "feet." Jim designed this paper collage illustration for a proposal for a live performance of the Muppets at New York's Lincoln Center. *Java* was first performed on *The Ed Sullivan Show*. It exhibited the innocence and charm for which Henson's comedy sketches were so well known. Here the small hose watches the dance steps the large hose is performing. Then he tries to mimic the dance steps. When the small hose masters the dance steps, his exuberance takes over and he dances at breakneck speed. The larger hose doesn't like being upstaged, so he shoves him off the stage and continues to dance. The small hose timidly sidesteps his way back on stage. Wearing a sweet, innocent expression, he watches the bigger hose closely and gets into synch with his dance steps. When the small hose gets the hang of it, they finish the dance together. On the last note, the small hose lifts one foot and blows his large cousin off the stage. Then he does a jubilant victory dance. For Henson, who believed there was strength in innocence, his innocent characters often triumph over the bullies. The audience forgives the shooting of the big hose because deep down everyone wants to be rid of the bully. This David-versus-Goliath philosophy is found in much of Jim's work, especially in his work with monsters. Moreover, here's another example of Henson's philosophy of reducing to bare essentials with particularly simple visual elements.

Java, illustration for a proposal for *The Muppets at Lincoln Center*. c. 1972. Marker and paper collage, 8½ x 11"

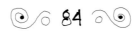

Things Get Hairy: Muppet Monsters

As he got older, Henson moved from drawing dragons to drawing monsters, which he used to represent fear, obsession, and other kinds of shameless behavior. One comedy sketch that appeared on *The Ed Sullivan Show* has Kermit reading aloud from a sheet of music on top of a piano that says, "Music hath charm to soothe the savage beast." Instantly, a savage beast appears and Kermit pacifies him by playing lively versions of *Tea for Two* and *You Must Have Been a Beautiful Baby*. A larger beast appears next, followed by an even larger beast. Kermit plays for his life to soothe all the beasts. When he has quieted the last one, he takes a bow–only to be eaten by the piano, which has turned into a monster. Jim also enjoyed unexpected endings, and sometimes he would turn a sketch upside down and sacrifice the hero.

Opposite: *Monster with Big Eyes*, puppet design. Late 1970s. Pencil, 11 x 8½"

Below: *Flower-Eating Monster*, puppet design for an appearance on *The Julie Andrews Show*. 1975. Pencil, 24 x 17¼"

"Who would have thought a good little girl like you could destroy my beautiful wickedness!"

—The Wicked Witch of the West, from *The Wizard of Oz.*

Henson used innocence, purity, and a sharp wit to destroy ferocious monsters. Consider his sketchbook drawing for a comedy piece featuring a little girl and a monster. A more refined version of the same piece is also pictured here. In six frames, Jim uses images alone to convey the story of a girl outwitting a monstrous fear. A script was recently found in the company archives that shows the thinking behind this sketch.

Jim never produced this version on television, but a similar idea called *Beautiful Day* was produced. In this rendition, the little girl points out several reasons why it's a beautiful day. A dreadful monster reverses all her declarations, one by one. He eats her beautiful flower. He smashes her beautiful flowerpot. He shoots the beautiful bird flying by. He even makes it rain on her beautiful day. When the little girl can no longer ignore the monster, she turns to him and says, "You're perfectly awful. You're so perfectly awful, it's beautiful." When the monster thinks his awfulness might be beautiful, he begins to shrink. The more the little girl praises him for having perfected the art of beautiful awfulness, the more the monster shrinks. He becomes smaller and smaller until the girl pulls out a fly swatter and squashes what's left of him. Triumphant, she declares: "You gotta talk your problems down to a size where you can handle 'em!"

Jim believed fear only had the power that one gave to it, and he shared his philosophy through puppetry and humor. "All of this stuff is about mankind trying to see himself in perspective. It's trying to figure out what you are and what you're doing here."

Opposite: *Girl and Monster*, sketchbook drawings for a possible variety-show appearance. Mid-1960s. Marker, 8½ x 5½" (each page)

Pages 90–91
Frame 1: Hi, there. My name is Betsy Marcella Lewellyn Fortesque. I'm never afraid of anything, because I won't let myself think of anything as being scary.

Frame 2: Now if you didn't like fuzzy wiggly things, for instance, you might not like this thing. Hello nice, fuzzy little thing. . . . (It snorts up to her and sniffs around.)

Frame 3: You must not let yourself be afraid here, because if you become afraid here, you better run for it. Help!

Frame 4: Oh, no! You can see how panic has a detrimental effect on the situation. You see, this thing is nowhere near as bad as I think it is. (It laughs at her.) Matter of fact, this beast is probably some harmless little fuzzy creature that my imagination wants me to believe is going to (in sudden fear) EAT ME UP! (Monster makes licking-of-chops kind of hungry noises.)

Frame 5: Wait a minute! (Monster stops in surprise.) You should find something else to eat. Hey, here's something nice and fuzzy to eat. Well, go ahead. Eat it.

Frame 6: Monster starts eating and eventually eats itself up entirely. Funny line inserted here.

Girl and Monster, revised sketch of a variety show appearance idea. Mid-1960s. Marker, 11 x 8½"(each page)

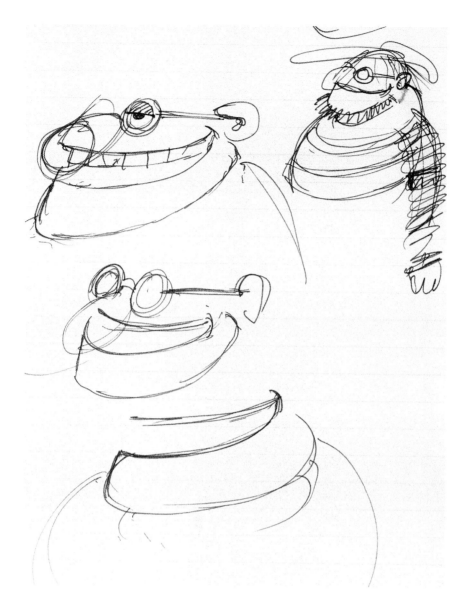

Dr. Teeth, puppet design for *The Muppet Show.* 1974. Ink, 11 x 8½"

Dr. Teeth

In 1974 Henson drew a sketch for a puppet known as *Dr. Teeth,* who was the leader of The Electric Mayhem, *The Muppet Show*'s famous house band. Performed by Jim, Dr. Teeth was based on New Orleans singer and musician Dr. John. In Jim's drawing, Dr. Teeth wears a pair of round wire-rimmed glasses à la John Lennon. The finished puppet sported upside-down dark glasses, a beaded necklace, an orange-and-blue striped shirt, and a furry pink top hat with a matching striped fringe vest. The "X" on his tooth in the drawing became Dr. Teeth's gold tooth on the show. He would also have a green face, with orange hair, orange beard, and orange nose.

Dr. Teeth spoke in a deep, gravelly voice and said such things as, "I'll melt down my records and put 'em in my teeth." His band members included Zoot on saxophone, Animal on drums, Floyd Pepper on bass, and Janice on vocals, tambourine, and left-handed guitar. The Electric Mayhem made their debut on "Sex and Violence," the 1975 pilot for *The Muppet Show.*

Flutes, Wheels, and Crown Monsters

In 1966 Henson drew three monsters that appeared in a General Foods commercial that featured three crunchy snack foods, Wheels, Crowns, and Flutes. Each snack was represented by a different monster. The Wheel-Stealer was a short, fuzzy monster with wonky eyes and sharply pointed teeth. The Flute-Snatcher was a speed demon with a long, sharp nose and windblown hair. The Crown-Grabber was a hulk of a monster with a Boris Karloff accent and teeth that resembled giant knitting needles.

These monsters had insatiable appetites for the snack foods they were named after. Each time the Muppet narrator, a human-looking fellow, fixes himself a tray of Wheels, Flutes, and Crowns, they disappear before he can eat them. One by one, the monsters sneak in and zoom away with the snacks. Frustrated and peckish, the narrator warns viewers that these pesky monsters could be disguised as someone in your own home, at which point the monsters briefly turn into people and then dissolve back to monsters again.

Henson used these monsters to illustrate familiar human impulses, exaggerating their behavior to point out the analogy. And the Wheel-Stealer puppet evolved into *Sesame Street's* Cookie Monster.

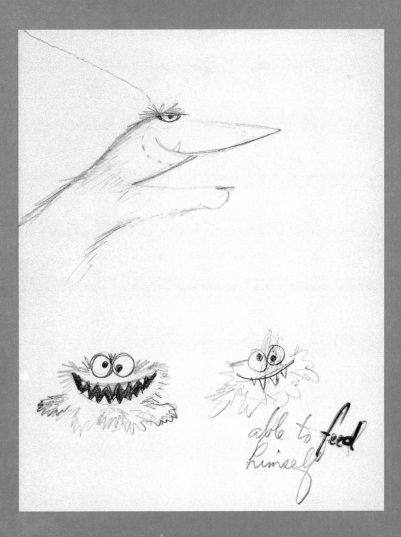

Flute Snatcher and Wheel Stealer, puppet designs for a General Foods snack food commercial. 1966. Pencil, 11⅛ x 7⅞"

HOOT

BA-BA

CROAK   SWEEP

Cover page from an early proposal for *The Muppet Show*. 1968. Marker, photo collage, and typewriting, 11 x 8½"

THAT'S ENTERTAINMENT!

Bird, character sketch for *Sesame Street.* 1970. Marker, 8½"x 5½"

"What Jim really wanted to do was to sing songs and tell stories, teach children, promote peace, save the planet, celebrate man, praise God and be silly."

—Jerry Juhl

The Way to Sesame Street

In 1968 Joan Ganz Cooney, founder of Children's Television Workshop, approached Henson about featuring the Muppets in an experimental children's television show. She envisioned teaching concepts to children with things that they already liked, such as animated cartoons, puppetry, TV commercials, game shows, catchy songs, and humor. She also wanted children to learn about cultural diversity as well as family and community values. It was a revolutionary idea for a children's show, and Henson liked it. Even so, he resisted the offer at first, fearing the Muppets would lose their adult audience. Yet the opportunity suited his talents and interests exactly. Plus, he had worked with other members of the team, such as Jon Stone and Joe Raposo, whom he respected. Jim knew how to make funny commercials; he had experience in animated film, puppetry, and in creating musical numbers. It was clear this partnership would allow him to continue developing these interests. And with children of his own at home, creating an entertaining children's show the whole family could enjoy was particularly enticing.

Henson brought wit, charm, joy, intelligence, and boundless energy to the *Sesame Street* Muppets, just as he had to his other work. He discovered that what applied to the adult audience applied to the preschool audience as well. Some of his best ideas came from his own children. "He loved their senses of humor," Jane Henson said. "And he would turn to them to find out what was funny."

"Sesame Street is an extraordinary story about how an experiment just took off and became part of the very fabric of our culture." —

—Michael Frith, former director of creative services, Jim Henson Productions, Inc.

Bird, character sketches for
Sesame Street. 1970. Marker,
8½" x 5½" (each page)

These are the People in Your Neighborhood

Jim Henson's idea for a big bird goes back to 1963 when he sketched Gourmet Bird for a Stouffer's frozen-food commercial. At the time Jim was experimenting with full-costume puppets, so to help visualize how the puppet would work he illustrated a view of the puppeteer inside the puppet. The puppeteer would have to hold one arm over his head to operate the beak, while the other arm would slip into a sleeve of feathers for the wing. A scribble through one of the puppeteer's arms shows Jim's thought process as he figured out where the second arm should go. For the puppeteer to see where he was going, he would look out from a scrim in the bird's neck. The bird's legs and webbed feet would be pulled on like a pair of socks. One new detail, indicated in the margin, are eyes that blinked. Although this commercial was never produced, Jim revisited this idea in 1969, when he did a color sketch for the real Big Bird. In this drawing, Big Bird looks like a slightly slimmer version of the character he is today.

Then in 1970 Jim drew a backward bird. The puppeteer was meant to stand inside the costume backward with his knees bent in order to imitate the bend of a real bird's legs. "That is *so* Jim," Jerry Juhl said recently. "It's just the kind of thing Jim loved. 'Wait a minute!' he used to say. 'We can do this!'" Jim would do anything to make an illusion appear more believable. A close look at backward bird reveals a vague outline of the puppeteer inside the costume. Facing backward also meant the puppeteer would have to operate the puppet from behind. The possibilities for stumbling were endless. In the end the idea for backward bird was dropped, not because operating the puppet was too awkward, but because the costume was too heavy.

In 1969 Jim sketched rough drawings for the characters of Ernie and Bert, and passed them along to his colleague and gifted puppet builder Don Sahlin. From Jim's quick

Gourmet Bird, puppet design for a Stouffer's frozen-food commercial. 1963. Pencil, 11 x 8½"

EXHIBIT A

Above: *Big Bird,* puppet design
for *Sesame Street.* 1969. Pencil
and marker, 13¼ x 11"

Right: *Standing Bird,*
full-body puppet design.
1970s. Pencil, 11 x 8½"

scribbles, Don captured the essence of these two characters, giving them their simple, classic look. Ernie has a wide, horizontal shape, whereas Bert is narrow and vertical. And their personalities are as different as the direction of the stripes on their shirts. Ernie is enthusiastic about everything, from taking a bath to imagining taking a trip to the moon. Bert is straightlaced and boring; he likes to collect paper clips and bottle caps. Ernie teases and torments Bert constantly. He turns the TV on when Bert is reading. He counts sheep out loud when Bert is trying to sleep. One time he used Bert's cowboy boot for a fishbowl. Ernie and Bert have been compared to comedy teams such as Laurel and Hardy, Burns and Allen, and Abbott and Costello. Just like their predecessors, Ernie and Bert drive each other crazy, and they are the best of friends. Jim and Frank Oz, who performed Ernie and Bert, were the greatest of friends too. Sometimes they would laugh so hard on the set they cried. Their sense of fun and horseplay came through in the characters as two dear ol' pals.

Sesame Street would go on to win seventy-one Emmys, eight Grammys, and the hearts of children and families all around the world, making the Muppets a household name. It was the street that paved the way to some of Jim's greatest projects, including *The Muppet Show,* Muppet movies, and a successful production company with offices in New York, Los Angeles, and London.

Opposite: *Bert as Gene Shalit,* puppet design for an appearance on *The Today Show,* April 4, 1974. Pencil, $8^3/_4$ x $6^3/_4$ "

Short, round creatures, puppet designs. 1960s. Pencil and ink on paper, 14 x $8^1/_2$ "

The Muppet Workshop

Big Bird's feathered torso and orange legs dangle from the ceiling; Grover and Elmo stand propped on wire hat stands; a family of foam pigs hangs from a rack of wooden pegs. Foam noses in boxes look like exotic fruit. Jewels, pearls, and sequins along with beads, buttons, and plastic eyeballs fill jars, baskets, and plastic containers. Drawers brim with fur, fleece, feathers, claws, and beaks. Drafting boards and tables are strewn with wigs, foam, plastic bones, and webbing. An animated loaf of bread stares from a shelf while a giant, foam chocolate chip cookie hangs on the wall like a clock. This is where the Muppets come from—Jim Henson's Muppet Workshop in New York City.

The artisans who design, build, and repair the Muppets at the workshop often talk and joke about the characters as they work, speculating where characters might live, whether they eat spaghetti from the can, or what their childhoods may have been like. These discussions often contribute to a character's personality. It's not unusual to see faceless Muppets propped here and there, waiting to be given an identity. These blank-looking Muppets are known as Anything Muppets or Whatnots and can be transformed into a fireman, a symphony conductor, or a trapeze artist at a moment's notice.

Crafting and costuming each Muppet calls for great attention to detail. The miniature shoes for a pirate are carefully distressed to look tattered and worn. When the Muppet rats sing and dance an Irish jig, they wear authentic looking, hand-knit fisherman's sweaters. Henson took great pleasure in the fine details of building the Muppets, from Miss Piggy's designer wardrobe to the miniature snowmobiles ridden by a band of creatures in "Emmet Otter's Jug-Band Christmas." "He always believed that what went on the screen had to be of superior quality. And all the money went on the screen and usually then some," said Jerry Juhl.

Jim loved working with the other artists at the workshop, who were always coming up with creatures that were "unlike anything that had ever been seen before." He once said, "I like working collaboratively with people. At its best, the film and television world functions creatively this way. I have a terrific group of people who work with me, and I think of the work we do as 'our' work."

Opposite: *Ernie and Bert,* puppet designs for *Sesame Street.* 1969.
Top: marker, 8⅜ x 11", bottom: 8¾ x 11"

Oscar the Grouch, puppet
design for *Sesame Street.*
1969. Marker with acetate
overlay, 11 x 13¼ "

··•◊═══ Oscar the Grouch ═══◊•··

Oscar the Grouch was purple in Jim's original sketch. For his debut on *Sesame Street*, he had orange shag fur. Only during the show's second season did Oscar become green. In this early drawing, Henson explored Oscar's unpredictable temperament, seen in the different ways that he imagined how the puppet might move. The head could rise dramatically and unexpectedly when something riled Oscar, a technique similar to the rod extenders Jim used on his Snerf monsters of the late sixties as well as on Beaker. He also considered giving Oscar's body the ability to expand to make him appear suddenly threatening. For a sly and crafty look, Jim rendered Oscar flat and low to the ground, making him appear inconspicuous, ready to strike, and watchful.

    Oscar's favorite expression became "Scram!" and Jim made sure that the puppet's body language said the same thing. He gave Oscar a glaring stare, together with prickly, "don't touch me" fur. Every child knows what it's like to feel crabby, and Oscar shows how funny and ridiculous it is to be perpetually grouchy. Like all the Muppets on *Sesame Street*, Oscar appeals to an adult's sense of humor as well. Played by puppeteer Caroll Spinney for over thirty years, Oscar displays a bad mood so delightfully that it often breaks the spell of a rotten day.

In 1969 Henson created an intricately designed proposal for a show called *Johnny Carson and the Muppet Machine*. Full of mischievous Muppet faces, peering from nooks and crannies and from behind cogs, buttons, and smokestacks, it was a concept for a half-hour television special, starring Johnny Carson. Reflecting on this proposal recently, Jerry Juhl laughed and commented, "What were we thinking? Johnny Carson would never have considered playing a straight man!" Seven panels illustrate a hilarious and harrowing journey inside a Muppet machine. Although this show was never produced, it showed Jim's delight in spoofing the "machine age." In the sixties machines were often looked upon with distrust, as though they would be capable of taking over the world. Jim poked fun at man and his machines, because both were prone to making mistakes. The flip side to this is that although Henson depicted monsters gobbling up computers, he was also fascinated by new technology and worked with clients such as IBM.

Opposite: Cover design for a proposal for a television special, *Johnny Carson and the Muppet Machine*. c. 1968–69. Facsimile, 11 x 8½"

Don Music

Don Music, puppet design for *Sesame Street*. 1980s. Pencil, 11 x 8½"

Don Music, a ridiculous character that Henson created for *Sesame Street*, was a frustrated songwriter performed by Richard Hunt. Don always had trouble getting his lyrics right. Sitting at the piano he would sing out the letters of the alphabet, but part way through he would forget what came next. "Oh, I'll never get this song right, never, never, never!" he would wail as he banged his head against the piano in frustration. Kids thought Don was very funny and some of them even imitated his head banging. Soon Children's Television Workshop began to receive complaints from parents, and Don Music was dropped from the cast. An Anything Muppet, he also appeared as Guy Smiley, *Sesame Street*'s fast-talking game show host. Performed by Jim, Guy was the epitome of the American game show host—shallow, loud, and wildly enthusiastic. He hosted such shows as *The Triangle is Right* and *Squeal of Fortune*.

This versatile Muppet appeared in other sketches as well. He once played Prince Charming in a skewed version of *Rapunzel*, in which Rapunzel speaks in a thick New York accent and wears a golden wig. Instead of letting down her hair, she throws down the wig, revealing her bald head. Horrified, Prince Charming flees the set as Kermit, *Sesame Street*'s on-the-spot reporter, breaks the story.

JOHNNY CARSON
AND
THE MUPPET MACHINE

BY...

JERRY JUHL

AND

JIM HENSON

a concept for a half-hour

television special

Illustrations for a proposal
for a television special,
*Johnny Carson and the
Muppet Machine.* c. 1968–69.
Facsimile, 11 x 8½"

Panel One: Johnny arrives at the studio to appear in a show he knows nothing about. The only thing in the studio is a machine covered with buttons, levers, and gauges. Johnny pushes a button marked "Start." The machine comes to life and begins to give Johnny instructions.

Panel Two: Johnny is told to walk through a door, pictured at the top of the panel. Reluctantly, he obeys the machine. The door leads into a stone tunnel leading to two more doors. Along the way, the machine warns Johnny to obey its instructions and to beware of the frightful monsters called Fearzogs. Johnny proceeds through one of the two doors shown at the bottom of the panel and winds up in the land of the Kazeeziks.

Panel Four: Johnny winds up in a cave with talking stalagmites and stalactites. Continuing along, he comes to an open plain, where he encounters a talking boulder bearing the image of Ed McMahon. Throughout the journey, Johnny and the machine trade a stream of insults. Soon Johnny meets up with a character, pictured at the bottom of the panel, named Haviland P. Squill, a shaggy fur-clad Muppet with the demeanor of an "oily carnival pitchman." This character pops in periodically to sell useless items to Johnny.

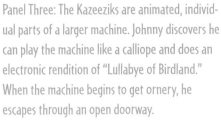

Panel Three: The Kazeeziks are animated, individual parts of a larger machine. Johnny discovers he can play the machine like a calliope and does an electronic rendition of "Lullabye of Birdland." When the machine begins to get ornery, he escapes through an open doorway.

111

Illustrations for a proposal for a television special, *Johnny Carson and the Muppet Machine*. c. 1968–69. Facsimile, 11 x 8½"

Panel Five: Shown at the top of this panel are a few of the items Haviland P. Squill has sold to Johnny, including an Edsel hubcap, a ticket to the 1937 World Series, and four pounds of spiced yak butter. The proposal suggests Johnny will find uses for each item. Below the items are characters called The Groans. Every time Johnny tells a bad joke, the Groans leap from the cracks in the wall and groan with pain. At the bottom of the panel, Johnny runs into a hairy, toothsome Fearzog. Moments later, he is being prepared as the Fearzogs' main course for dinner. The chief Fearzog thumbs through a cookbook called *1000 Ways to Prepare TV Stars*.

Panel Six: Fortunately, Haviland Squill is disguised as the assistant chef and has a box that holds the answer to escaping Fearzogs, but it will cost Mr. Carson $14.95. Johnny is short on cash, but being in a bit of a bind, he decides to write a check. He opens the box and pulls out a piece of paper that simply says, "Run!" Johnny runs, pursued by the Fearzogs.

Illustration for a proposal for a television special, *Johnny Carson and the Muppet Machine*. c. 1968–69. Facsimile, 11 x 8½"

Panel Seven: Crashing down a chute, Johnny returns to the studio where the journey began. "Thank you, Mr. Carson, you have just completed the tour," the Muppet Machine says. As the credits roll, the machine blows up and Haviland P. Squill is shown sweeping up the debris as the proposal comes to a close.

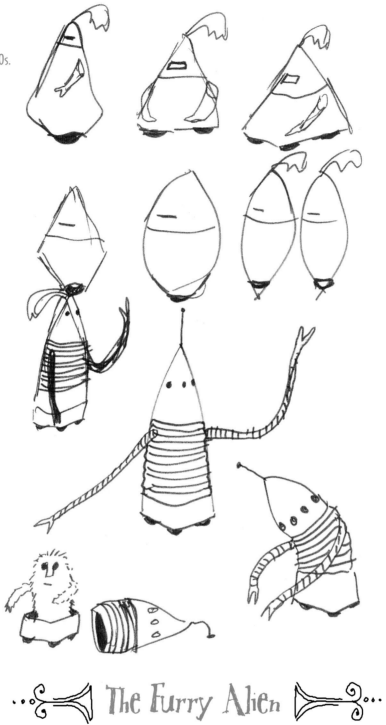

Alien, character sketch from a sketchbook. 1960s. Marker, 8½ x 5½"

···ꙮ The Furry Alien ꙮ···

According to Jerry Juhl and Bonnie Erickson, Jim truly believed that "the meek would inherit the earth." A doodle of an alien from a 1960s sketch reveals this. As this mechanical character evolves, it seems to become aware that it is encumbered. It rolls on its four wheels, lifts its twisty arms, and then crumples over, freeing itself from the metal canister in which it has been bound. Behind the robot mask–at the heart of its being–is a sweet, furry creature. Henson not only had an ability to create disguises but also had the ability to remove them. Jim believed that behind the social mask every human being wears there was an innate goodness, purity, and meekness. An adjunct to his great creative talent was his ability to recognize, appreciate, encourage, and celebrate individuality. Bernie Brillstein, his long-time business manager and friend, once said that Jim was able to "find greatness in difference."

Above: *Dog*, puppet design.
Late 1970s. Pencil, 11 x 8½"

Left: *Monsters with Horns*,
puppet designs. Early 1960s.
Pencil, 10¾ x 8⅛"

Henson loved the theater and considered doing a Broadway show that featured the Muppets. In 1971 he had developed several pieces that were performed live in a Las Vegas show hosted by Nancy Sinatra. He also toured with Jimmy Dean, which gave him a taste for live performance. The following year, Henson made a formal proposal to a group of theatrical producers to create a live revue to be performed at New York's Lincoln Center. Made of brightly colored cutout collage and marker drawings, this proposal had a more polished look than some of his earlier proposals. It contained images of earlier ideas, including *Sclrap Flyapp* and *Big Boss Man*, as well as concepts for new pieces, including *The Clodhoppers*, which were full-bodied, rod-operated puppets, and *Gawky Bird*, a colossal fifteen-foot rod puppet. In pieces that required special puppetry techniques, Jim indicated how a puppeteer would perform that particular puppet. The black forms seen in the backgrounds of *Big Boss Man, Gawky Bird*, and *The Clodhoppers* are puppeteers. The puppeteers had to wear black so they would be invisible to the audience during the performance. From the shadows, they operated the puppets with long rods connected to their bodies by a harness. These colossal puppets seemed to sing and dance by themselves, and actors and actresses could dance among them as well. The Muppets never made it to Broadway, but Jim always kept this idea in the back of his mind. As Jerry Juhl recalled, "Every couple of years, when Jim would take a week off, he would come in and say, 'We gotta do that Broadway show.'" Even today, the idea for a live show comes up for discussion in company production meetings. Perhaps the Muppets will "Take Manhattan" after all.

Opposite, top: *Gawky Bird*, illustration for a proposal for *The Muppets at Lincoln Center*. c. 1972. Marker and paper collage, 8½" x 11"

Opposite, bottom: *Big Boss Man*, illustration for a proposal for *The Muppets at Lincoln Center*. c. 1972. Marker and paper collage, 8½ x 11"

Below: *The Clodhoppers*, illustration for a proposal for *The Muppets at Lincoln Center*. c. 1972. Marker and paper collage, 8½ x 11"

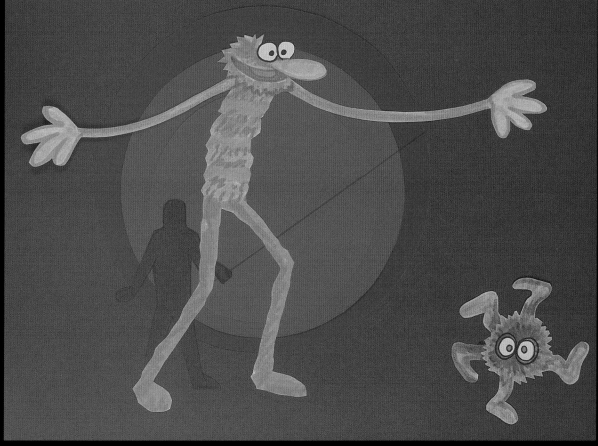

Left: *Thog*, sketch for Nancy Sinatra's Las Vegas show. 1971. Ink, 8¾ x 5⅞"

Below: *Big Boss Man*, puppet design for Nancy Sinatra's Las Vegas show. 1971. Ink and marker, 8¾ x 12"

Sclrap Flyapp, Koozebanians, and Snerfs, illustration for a proposal for *The Muppets at Lincoln Center.* c. 1972. Marker and paper collage, 8½ x 11"

East 69th Street

The home office of the Muppets is located on Manhattan's Upper East Side in a 1920s neo-Federal period townhouse. The Muppets also have offices in Los Angeles and London, but the New York office reflects Jim's creative and familial approach to business. He bought this building in 1977, during *The Muppet Show* years. Featured inside the front door is a display case with the latest Muppet creation. In the foyer, the receptionist sits behind a semi-circular wooden counter, inlaid with hand-carved Muppet characters. To the left of the receptionist, a floor-to-ceiling mural features the entire cast of *The Muppet Show*. A waiting area directly in front of this mural contains a row of theater seats from a torn-down suburban playhouse. The word "ha!" appears in brass letters on the foyer's marble floor. These letters stood for Henson Associates, which the company was called during the 1980s.

From the lobby, a grand spiral staircase winds up three floors, where a smaller spiral staircase leads to the fourth floor. Not only did Jim love the way this staircase looked, he thought it provided easy communication among employees. He described it as a "huge, vertical telephone." Jim didn't like the idea of employees separated by floors, and the staircase made a natural open line of communication.

Homey, artistic details characterize Henson's company headquarters. To him, work, home, and family were intertwined. He selected the furniture from galleries around the world. Fresh flowers still greet employees and visitors in the lobby. Hanging in the fourth floor spiral stairwell's shaft is an intricate wire, wood, and metal sculpture entitled the "Great Hot Air Balloon Race," which Jim had commissioned for this space from his younger son, John, and sculptor John Kahn. Miniature Muppets cling to the wires, performing a circus show for all four floors. Muppets also appear on the ceiling at the top of the building in a stained-glass window called "View from the Lily Pad," and the wallpaper in the lobby's bathroom shows a Muppets print. Even the elevator shaft has a shaggy blue monster painted on the wall that peeks through the metal accordion doors on the way to the fourth floor. Jim once said, "I don't want a pretentious space or one with a feeling of opulence. Instead, I want a happy, functioning space with character and warmth." This feeling still prevails at the home office of the Muppets today.

Illustration for *The Muppet Show* proposal. 1972. Marker and typewriting, 11 x 8½"

In 1968 Jim designed a cover proposal for *The Muppet Show* with colored markers (page 96). Pasted to the bottom of the page is a black-and-white cutout photo of an early, pre-frog Kermit. Unlike most highly polished proposals submitted for a prime-time, big-budget television show, this one had the homespun feel of a handmade birthday card or a school book report cover. *The Muppet Show* proposal reflected Jim Henson's style—unpretentious on the outside, brilliant visionary on the inside.

The Muppet Show proposal included a rough description of the show's content. Jim envisioned a half-hour, prime-time variety show that would feature short sketches such as the Seven Deadly Sins personified, a guru who predicts the future by reading the distribution of mushrooms on a pizza, and a long-running poker game that parodies the Vietnam War. Suggestions for whimsical musical numbers, such as musician Donovan performing with a four-headed monster rock band called *The Big Four,* were also included in the proposal. The show would feature a weekly guest star, different styles of puppetry, satiric pieces, and its own cast of creatures, animals, monsters, machines, and abstract things. Jim called it a family show: The humor would appeal to adults, and children would enjoy the puppetry and musical numbers. Henson described *The Muppet Show* as "a fast-paced, uninhibited, free-form farce." He believed the "time was right for a variety show hosted by dogs, frogs, and monsters."

The Muppet Show did find its proper venue, but it took another visionary, British entertainment mogul Lord Lew Grade, to recognize the originality and potential of Jim's proposal. In 1976 Lord Grade approved production of twenty-four episodes of *The Muppet Show* at his studios in England. When *The Muppet Show* first aired in 1976, it was an instant success. For the next five seasons, it would appear in more than one hundred countries. Jim also produced three movies with Lord Grade's production company: *The Muppet Movie, The Great Muppet Caper,* and *The Muppets Take Manhattan.* Jim Henson had waited over ten years to find a home for *The Muppet Show*—it was certainly worth the wait.

In the early days of the company, Henson designed his own holiday greeting cards. Jim valued his friends and associates, and he liked to show his appreciation in creative, personal ways. *A Joyful Yuletide,* drawn in 1956, shows a jolly bearer of Christmas tidings, similar to the long, narrow forms in his silkscreen prints of the same period.

In a 1957 Christmas card called *Holiday Greetings,* Jim featured Yorick, the skull-shaped monster known for his insatiable appetite, who gained notoriety after eating Kermit on *Sam and Friends* and later on *The Ed Sullivan Show.* Here, Yorick, wearing his perpetually comical and infernal grin, has eaten most of the Christmas tree, leaving behind a few denuded twigs, a star, and two lonely ornaments.

In 1969, at the height of the peace movement, Jim made his own anti-war statement, showing Kermit on the Muppet Christmas card sitting squarely in the middle of the word *Peace.* Henson believed that mankind had the ability to get along peaceably, and he encouraged this hope throughout his work. He once said, "I believe we can use television and film to be an influence for good; that we can help to shape the thoughts of children and adults in a positive way."

By 1971 *Sesame Street* was a well-established hit, and Big Bird received top billing on the company Christmas card. Looped in strings of lights, dotted with ornaments, and crowned with a star, Big Bird posed as the Christmas tree.

In addition to the handmade Christmas cards, Jim often made gifts for his friends. Sometimes he formed, baked, and shellacked cookie dough ornaments in the shapes of Muppet characters. For Frank Oz's birthday one year, Henson took the idea of a handmade gift one funny step further. He depicted Oz naked inside an elaborate model of *Sesame Street*'s Bert. When Jim bought gifts, he took special pains to pick out unusual and often handmade or antique objects for his family, friends, and associates. He had great respect for the people who worked for him. "Jim was the most giving man I've ever known," Frank Oz once said. "He had a great generosity of spirit, of time, and of money for other people. He valued quality work, but being a good human being was just as important to him."

Holiday Greetings, a Christmas card. 1957. Silkscreen, 2⅝ x 5⅜"

Right: *Peace*, a Christmas card, 1969. Lithograph, 3½ x 4¼"

Above: *Big Bird Christmas Tree*, a Christmas card. 1971. Handcolored lithograph, 7 x 5"

A Joyful Yuletide, a Christmas card. 1956. Silkscreen, 8¾ x 3¾"

···⚜ Early Chronology ⚜···

1936 Born September 24 in Greenville, Mississippi.

1954 Graduates from Northwestern High School and enters the University of Maryland.

First television appearance on *The Junior Morning Show*, WTOP/CBS, Washington, D.C.

1955 *Sam and Friends* begins airing live on WRC-TV, Washington, D.C.

1956 Appearances on *The Arthur Godfrey Show*, *The Steve Allen Show*, and *The Will Rogers, Jr. Show*.

1957 First Wilkins Coffee commercial taped.

1958 Travels to Europe; develops *Hansel and Gretel* upon return.

Sam and Friends wins a local Emmy award.

1959 Marries Jane Nebel.

1960 The Muppets appear for the first time on *The Today Show*, beginning regular appearances in 1961.

1962 *Tales of the Tinkerdee* is taped in Atlanta.

Rowlf is built by Don Sahlin for Purina Dog Chow commercial.

1963 The Muppets and the Henson family move to New York.

Rowlf begins regular appearances on *The Jimmy Dean Show*.

1964 *Time Piece* begins production.

1965 First meeting films are developed for IBM.

1966 Regular appearances on *The Ed Sullivan Show* begin, lasting until 1971.

The Muppets continue to make commercials for various clients including La Choy, FHA, Wilson's Meats, Southern Bell, and Royal Crown Cola.

First licensed products–Kermit, Rowlf, and Snerf dolls–are created with Ideal Toys.

1967 Begins Cyclia, an unrealized nightclub project.

1968 *Youth '68–NBC Experiment in Television*.

PBS special: *Muppets on Puppets*.

Hey, Cinderella! filmed in Toronto.

1969 *The Cube–NBC Experiment in Television*.

Sesame Street begins first season.

1970 TV special: *The Great Santa Claus Switch*.

1971 Muppet guest appearances on *The Flip Wilson Show*, the *Goldie Hawn Special*, the *Dick Cavett Special*, and others.

TV special: *The Frog Prince*.

Muppets are featured in Nancy Sinatra's Las Vegas nightclub act.

1972 TV special: *Muppet Musicians of Bremen*.

1973 *Muppet Valentine Special* with Mia Farrow.

1974 Muppet guest appearances on *The Tonight Show*, *The Today Show*, *What's My Line?*, and others.

1975 "Sex and Violence," TV series pilot for the *The Muppet Show*.

Muppets guest appearances on the *Cher TV Special*, *The Mike Douglas Show*, *The Julie Andrews Show*, and others.

Weekly appearances on *Saturday Night Live*'s first season.

1976 *The Muppet Show* first season ... and the rest is history.

Compiled by Karen Falk